Praise for *Leading School Teams*

If you are a school or district administrator with the time, energy, and courage to take on the major concerns of your school/district and are willing to implement a plan with possible systemic change, then this book is for you.

—Jim Anderson
Principal, Andersen Jr. High School

In order for any team or change effort to be successful, relational trust is key. In Leading School Teams, *Dave Horton offers practical strategies to enhance relational trust in order to transform adult-centered systems into systems that put students at the center!*

—Paul Bloomberg, EdD
Chief Learning Officer
The Core Collaborative

Building effective teams at all levels of an organization is critical for long-term success. Nowhere is this more evidenced than in the principal coaching I do, where building vital relationships and high-performing teams transcends traditional content and data and gets to the heart of what we value in one another and our collective work. Dr. Horton has laid out a comprehensive— and palatable—approach to teaming that values the individual strengths of each stakeholder and lays the foundation for teacher enthusiasm and learner engagement.

—Dr. Michael Roe
Principal, Riverside Poly High School

This year I was faced with the challenge of starting a brand-new community day school, changing the paradigm of how we educate expelled and at-risk youth, and implementing curriculum and procedures that are truly new and innovative choices for our teachers. As I read through Leading School Teams, *I saw a few specific topics that I felt were key discussions to have as a fledgling staff, but sometimes folks can be hesitant in truly being honest about difficult topics. One of the best discussions we were able to have was in regard to the following prompt from Chapter 7 of* Leading School Teams: *"Do we have a system to collect data on the program or initiative? Is it simple to use and simple to understand? Have results targets been determined before the program launch?" This prompt was able to facilitate a powerful discussion on how we are evaluating our progress, and how effectively we are meeting targets that we set at the outset of the year. As a staff we are looking forward to continuing these discussions using the same format and seeing the growth that will come from vibrant and honest discussions.*

—Cristian Miley
Principal, ASPIRE Community Day School

The strategies within Leading School Teams *allowed our leadership team to develop a deeper understanding between our members. This enabled our team to create more effective connections with each other, improved our levels of communication, and strengthened our team's bond.*

—Jeff Franks
Principal, Acacia Middle School

Whether you are a new leader of a team, an established team in need of trust or a culture shift, a team where not everyone's voice is heard, or a team without established systems, Leading School Teams *provides the tools needed to create a highly effective team. This book provides powerful insight to practical activities that can be easily implemented with any team, at any stage, with an end result of productive change. Diagnose your team, engage in the activities and dialogue, and watch your team transform.*

—Leah C. Davis
Executive Director of Riverside County SELPA

Chapter 4 of Leading School Teams allowed our team to address the lack of processes and the finger pointing and tension that went along with it. It was surprising how quickly the activities and discussion brought out the meat of the issues within our team. It happened in a natural way that it snuck up on the team, and we were in the middle of addressing the real issues before we realized what was happening. Additionally, because of the natural manner in which the issues were approached, team members felt respected and accomplished after each session.

—Eric Dahlstrom
Principal, Dartmouth Middle School

This book provides leaders and teams with a blueprint of how to work through a problem to find possible solutions while valuing each member of the team. This is not an easy task at any level, and to have a resource to provide guidance for those tough situations is always welcomed.

—Nicky Kemp
Assistant Superintendent, North Callaway R-1 School District

To those who believe that the all of us is stronger than the one of us.

Leading School Teams

Building Trust to Promote Student Learning

David M. Horton

CORWIN
A SAGE Publishing Company

FOR INFORMATION:

Corwin

A SAGE Company

2455 Teller Road

Thousand Oaks, California 91320

www.corwin.com

SAGE Ltd.

1 Oliver's Yard

55 City Road

London EC1Y 1SP

United Kingdom

SAGE Pvt. Ltd.

B 1/I 1 Mohan Cooperative Industrial Area

Mathura Road, New Delhi 110 044

India

SAGE Publications Asia-Pacific Pte. Ltd.

3 Church Street

#10-04 Samsung Hub

Singapore 049483

Executive Editor: Arnis Burvikovs

Senior Associate Editor: Desirée A. Bartlett

Senior Editorial Assistant: Andrew Olson

Production Editor: Veronica Stapleton Hooper

Copy Editor: Terri Lee Paulsen

Typesetter: C&M Digitals (P) Ltd.

Proofreader: Ellen Howard

Indexer: Jeanne R. Busemeyer

Cover Designer: Anupama Krishnan

Marketing Manager: Anna Mesick

ISBN: 978-1-5063-4492-8

This book is printed on acid-free paper.

16 17 18 19 20 10 9 8 7 6 5 4 3 2 1

Contents

Acknowledgments

I would like to thank the many teams and professionals who have allowed me to observe, contribute, and share in their journey. This book and its message would not be possible without them. I would also like to thank Arnis, Desirée, and Andrew on the Corwin team, who helped this book from its earliest days to its final steps in the development process. It couldn't have happened without them. And finally, I would like to thank my wife and children for their support and patience. They make it worth the sacrifice of time and energy.

PUBLISHER'S ACKNOWLEDGMENTS

Corwin gratefully acknowledges the contributions of the following reviewers:

Lydia Adegbola
Assistant Principal
Legacy School for Integrated Studies
New York, New York

Jim Anderson
Principal
Andersen Jr. High School
Chandler, Arizona

Laurie Barron
Superintendent
Evergreen School District
Kalispell, Montana

Jason Ellingson
Superintendent
Collins-Maxwell CSD
Maxwell, Iowa

Rich Hall
Director of Elementary Education
Henrico County Public Schools
Henrico, Virginia

Freda Hicks
Principal
Perry Harrison Elementary School
Pittsboro, North Carolina

Nicky Kemp
Assistant Superintendent
North Callaway R-1 School District
Kingdom City, Missouri

Lynn Lisy-Macan
Visiting Assistant Professor
University at Albany—SUNY
Albany, New York

Theresa M. Marshall
Associate Principal
Carver Elementary School
Henrico, Virginia

About the Author

 David M. Horton is a life-long educator. He has served as an assistant superintendent of Educational Services, a K–12 director of Curriculum, Instruction, and Assessment; coordinator of Secondary Mathematics and K–12 Instructional Technology; high school assistant principal; and high school math and science teacher. David's area of expertise is building systems and structures of organizational leadership that align mission and vision with practice. He currently teaches as an adjunct professor with two Southern California universities.

David has a Bachelor of Science in Biology and Master of Education from the University of California, Los Angeles (UCLA). He received a Master of Science degree in Administration from Pepperdine University and earned a Doctor of Education degree in Organizational Leadership from the University of La Verne. David resides in Southern California with his wife and two children. David can be reached through his website, davidhortonwriter.com.

Introduction

SUSTAINED IMPROVEMENT REQUIRES TEAMS

Good news! This book has exactly what you need. Here, leaders and their teams will find the tools and processes they need to stay focused on (1) student learning, (2) the improvement of student learning, and (3) the successful sustainability of strategies and programs. The tools you find here will help you achieve all of those goals through teamwork, trust building, and collaborative behaviors.

This is a book for administrative leaders and their teams, and teacher leaders and their teams. The Activities herein create a space for educators to have team-building and capacity-building opportunities with the team members on a regular basis. This toolbox has two major advantages: (1) the activities are short, and (2) they require little to no preparation. The leader can simply ask the team to turn to a chosen page to begin the team-building conversation. Leaders often do not have the time to search out a group reading or activity that is diagnostically tailored to their teams' needs. Luckily, this book does that for them.

Most leaders and teams are committed professionals who value ideas, solutions, improvement, and team support. This process and system is designed for these sorts of people. It is for those who believe that teams are the most powerful component to sustained school and district improvement. John Hattie (2015) describes that the one strategy or behavior that improves student learning the most is "teacher collective efficacy." Consider this for a moment: Teachers, when they are collectively engaged in teaching, connecting with and caring for *all* students, and intensely focused on student learning and improvement, can do more to improve student learning than any other single strategy, behavior, or technique. In fact, Hattie (2015) reports that teacher collective efficacy improves student learning at a rate of four years of growth in one calendar year in schools where teacher collective efficacy is the norm and path of action.

Teacher Collective Efficacy

Four Years of Learning Growth in One Year

Brinson and Steiner (2007) note that principals can improve collective efficacy by

1. building instructional knowledge and skills,

2. creating opportunities for teachers to collaboratively share skills and experience,

3. interpreting results and providing actionable feedback on teachers' performance, and

4. involving teachers in school decision making.

Consider this list and reflect on how these goals might be achieved. For teachers to be collectively effective, they need teams so that they can come together and make connections. Teachers need the time and space that teams offer to discuss, share, fine-tune, plan, provide support, and coordinate efforts. It is difficult to think of achieving collective efficacy any other way.

So, if teacher collective efficacy is the most effective single strategy/ behavior/technique to experience the largest growth in student learning— and having teams is the most likely vehicle for teachers to do the work that makes them collectively effective—then leaders must do all they can to support teams at all levels. In other words, a leader cannot afford to have a team that is blocked, stuck, or unable to get to the work that allows them to be collectively effective.

This book is the toolset that leaders can use to set the stage, create the proper environment, build the trust, host the conversations, engage the members, and build the teams that can then focus on the actions that will make them more collectively effective. In other words, think of a meeting having two basic parts. The first half involves building trust, setting the tone, and engaging all team members. Then, in the second half, the team can get to the work described by Brinson and Steiner. The first step of setting the tone must be taken in order to be able to reach the collective efficacy needed to do the work of the second step.

Teams

Teacher Collective Efficacy

Four Years of Learning Growth in One Year

Each tool offered here has a unique and specialized purpose. Not every tool is needed for every team. Some teams may have very specific needs that lead them to a set of tools that may be very different from that of another team of comparable makeup.

To explore this concept of unique tools for unique teams, you will need to know how to use this book as well as how not to use it. Before delving into the chapters, please take the time to read the Introduction in its entirety, take the Quick-Start Diagnostic, and read through the Activity Guidelines carefully. You will then be able to find the right tool for the job at hand. Please refer to the Activity Guidelines as often as you need. Having them printed out next to you before you begin each Activity with your team would be a good idea.

WHAT THIS BOOK IS—WHAT THIS BOOK ISN'T

Years of observation, conversation with colleagues, sitting in team meetings, and the current thinking in organizational leadership went into the writing of this book. We know that most leaders are invested in the success of their teams. However, very often, leaders are missing the tools they need to (1) create teamwork, (2) engage team members, and (3) shepherd teams to succeed at devising solutions to the issues they wish to tackle. Think of this book as both a support and a vehicle. Use it to help your teams have the types of conversations that lead to discovering solutions and to better implementing the solutions they have already identified.

If your teams are operating well and all members are functional, then these tools may not be of immediate use. But when new team members arrive, established team members leave, or circumstances shift in other ways, then a tune-up on team dynamics can be helpful. That is where this book will be of great use.

There are some common behaviors or characteristics that teams display. The Conversation Prompts and Activities offered here will help team members better understand where they are, where they want to go, and how to get there. By providing assistance on an as-needed basis, this process will allow leaders to help their teams function better than they already do. Just like a home improvement project, not every tool in your toolbox will be needed for every project. Certain tools will just not be applicable to your circumstances. Some tasks require a wrench while other tasks call for a hammer. This doesn't mean that either tool is of lesser value. It just means that when you need a wrench, the hammer is not as critical to your present success. The various tools in this toolbox provide leaders with options they can tailor to their own particular needs. Regardless of the tool selected, the overall goal is to keep teams moving toward the collective efficacy that leads to the most learning for students.

This book is meant to be used in pieces, as needed for each team. It does not operate in isolation from other systems that may already be in place. If you already have structures in place such as Professional Learning Communities, Data Teams, or Impact Teams, for instance, these tools are designed to run parallel to those structures.

Leadership of Learning

As a leader, part of your job is leading the learning among not only your students, but your staff. Learning often begins by asking questions. Consider your school at this moment. I'm sure that without too much effort, you could rattle off a list of 10 things that you are very proud of because they are working and producing visible results. I am also certain you could list 10 more things that you would like to see improve. The nature of the game is an ever-changing landscape. Nothing remains static.

> ### 🔑 Key Thought
>
> "It is school leaders who promote challenging goals, and then establish safe environments for teachers to critique, question, and support other teachers to reach these goals together that have the most effect on student outcomes."
>
> —John Hattie—*Visible Learning* (2009), p. 83

For leaders and teams in this ever-changing environment, it becomes critical to understand the *why* behind the most important things going on in the school. Why are we continuing to do reading intervention this way? Why are the eighth-grade boys struggling with math? Why do our college prep classes have fewer students this year than last? By asking the *why* questions, many things can emerge. *Why* is a tough sentence starter. *Why* makes us dig. *Why* makes us dig deep. *Why* uncovers things.

> ### 🔑 Key Thought
>
> *Why* is a tough sentence starter. *Why* makes us dig. *Why* makes us dig deep. *Why* uncovers things.

Imagine a team that functions well enough together to ask the *why* questions routinely. Imagine a team that was cohesive enough to explore the reasons why some actions are producing results in the school while others are not. Imagine team members who could be as comfortable with troubling data and critical feedback as they are with celebrating the successes of the programs and initiatives that thrive. Imagine team members who understand their roles so well that they implement change not when it is best for the adults, but only when it will lead to improved student learning. If your team isn't in that place, what work can it do to achieve that level of efficacy and be comfortable enough to ask the *why* questions and do it in a productive manner, meeting after meeting?

Getting to Know Your Team

Leaders have schedules crammed with meetings that aim to cover unwieldy agendas. In most cases, however desirable it might be, it is not feasible to dedicate an entire meeting to team building, given the long list of demands from other pressing items. Therefore, the tools in this book are designed to be incorporated into existing meetings. The Application Activity tools take about 15 minutes to complete with your team, with the leader facilitating a conversation. Typically, there is one conversation prompt (Application Activity) to be used in any one 15-minute session. The conversation is designed to allow team members to talk and share their thoughts, feelings, beliefs, values, and experiences. The point and purpose of hosting these conversations is for team members to get to know each other on a much deeper level.

This book is ultimately about learning—student learning. We get there by improving the team dynamics that already exist in your school or district. **By choosing to improve the team dynamics, we hope to improve our collective efficacy.** And we know, being reminded by John Hattie, that collective efficacy does more to improve student learning than any other behavior or strategy.

QUICK-START DIAGNOSTIC

The diagnostic below includes a simple and quick series of questions that a leader can ask of herself to get a sense of her team's present location and needs. Once the leader obtains the results of the diagnostic, she can then use the cross-reference link to navigate to the section of the book that offers the most helpful tool for her team.

There are four different players who can benefit from this book and these tools: leaders, all teams, school learning teams, and district-level teams. The school learning team is any school-level team that has discussions about student learning (e.g., the Second-Grade Team, the Geometry Team). The district-level team is any district-level team of teachers, teacher representatives, and administrators who have oversight or direction over a program, support, instruction, curriculum, or assessment.

Read through the "IF—THEN" prompts below. As a leader, carefully consider the team you are focusing on. Consider the people, their strengths, their successes, their challenges, their logical steps for growth, and so on. Keeping these things in mind will help you select the best tool and conversation to move the team forward. Find the *best fit* descriptor for you and your team. There is no wrong answer. There is no wrong place to start. It is your perception of the most relevant needs of your team. The system is built to be used in a nonlinear, noncyclical format. You use what you or your team needs when they need it. There is no wrong way to get into this process.

MAKING A SELECTION

Read each of the prompts below. If you are doing this activity as a group, have a discussion regarding each prompt in the left column and do a force ranking to select one row that is *most* like your team. Lead the group to a conclusion about why that descriptor is most appropriate and that this will be the starting point that is most relevant for your team.

If you are . . .	Then . . .
. . . a new team with trust or basic team-building needs . . .	. . . start in Chapter 1.
. . . a new leader or the teams have had a great deal of movement . . .	. . . start in Chapter 1.
. . . a team that has not been trained on how to bring ideas forward . . .	. . . start in Chapter 2.
. . . a team that does not regularly self-reflect on how things get done . . .	. . . start in Chapter 2.
. . . already committed to a program or initiative but you have questions about its alignment to the "why" of the organization . . .	. . . start in Chapter 3.
. . . already committed to a program or initiative and you have questions about effectiveness and sustainability . . .	. . . start in Chapter 3.
. . . a team that has not discussed problem-solving strategies to give ongoing support to the program . . .	. . . start in Chapter 4.
. . . a team that is in need of trust, conflict, commitment, accountability, or results training or support . . .	. . . start in Chapter 4.
. . . a team in need of a culture and identity . . .	. . . start in Chapter 5.
. . . a team that does not yet understand the importance of diverse problem-solving styles on the team . . .	. . . start in Chapter 5.
. . . a team that needs support on the importance of norms to handle conflict . . .	. . . start in Chapter 5.
. . . a team that does not know the strengths of different team members to bring out relevant and timely points of view . . .	. . . start in Chapter 6.
. . . a team that does not have a process or habit to include everyone's voice based on strength and skill set . . .	. . . start in Chapter 6.
. . . a team with a program but no established system to collect and analyze data about the program . . .	. . . start in Chapter 7.

(Continued)

(Continued)

If you are . . .	Then . . .
. . . a team with a program but no established ongoing training, coaching, or feedback systems to support the program . . .	. . . start in Chapter 7.
. . . a team that does not or has not regularly self-examined for behaviors or habits that are known but silent productivity killers . . .	. . . start in Chapter 8.
. . . a team that has committed to "early" ideas without vetting them for fit and quality or doesn't maintain a process to be sure many ideas are considered . . .	. . . start in Chapter 8.
. . . a team that has a program or initiative selected but there is not a formal and active communication plan to support it . . .	. . . start in Chapter 9.
. . . a team that does not have established systems of feedback to monitor programs . . .	. . . start in Chapter 9.

Enter your selected Chapter Area of Focus here:

Chapter Area of Focus

IMPORTANT—Before you turn to the Area of Focus you wrote down, please finish reading the remainder of this section. It will help you understand the flow of how to manage the logistics of using your selection, do the team-building work, and then reassess your progress and make your next selection based on your team's current state.

PUTTING IT ALL TOGETHER

The process for continued use is a series of five basic steps.

1. Take the diagnostic.

2. Select a chapter area of focus.

3. In your selected chapter, look for prompts that most correspond to your needs.

4. Host the conversation—use the main topic.

5. Assess the team: Is there a benefit in continuing in the same Chapter Area of Focus? If yes, continue in current chapter. If no, return to the first step (the diagnostic).

At this point, you have already accomplished a few things. You know this book is meant to be used like a toolbox. It is not a book to start at page 1 and read from cover to cover. It is a set of resources to help leaders and teams develop so that deeper conversations and deeper solutions can be reached due to the teamwork, trust, and sharing that takes place.

You also used the Quick-Start Diagnostic to find a likely starting point. This gives you and your team a productive starting point that should have a targeted feel. Starting with this foundational work should yield a more personal and tailored discussion that will get the team moving and discussing important issues productively and efficiently.

Finally, you found how to use the tools as an iterative cycle. As soon as you have finished one tool or discussion you can use the Diagnostic to find the next discussion activity.

ACTIVITY GUIDELINES

Please review the Activity guidelines prior to each Activity.

Quick-Start Diagnostic: Although there is no wrong way to arrive at the conversations in the book, it is recommended that you begin by completing the Quick-Start Diagnostic in the beginning of the book to determine your individual team's most pressing need(s). Filling out the Quick-Start Diagnostic will offer valuable insights for all of the activities in the book.

Activity Prep: Before initiating each Activity, the leader should read through the entire Activity (and these Guidelines) to prepare for the needs of the team and the room. Have a plan for assigning the timekeeper and recorder. Assign other roles as needed. If people will be sharing with partners, have a plan for assigning partners to each other.

Scaffolding: It is not recommended to take on too much in the early stages of using these tools. Teams take time to develop and gather momentum. It is best to allow teams to acclimate to the discussions and the sharing. As time and experience build, teams and leaders will find that they can handle more content in shorter blocks of time.

Time: The Application Activities throughout the book are chunked in 15-minute increments (for a typical team of 6 to 8 people). Meaning, for a standard 60-minute meeting, this Team Development Activity would occupy the first 15 minutes of the meeting, unless you decide to continue with the additional prompts or extended activities. Any Application Activity can be extended by bringing in more content or discussion topics. One member of the team should take on the role of timekeeper (someone other than the facilitator) and monitor the time for the group.

Easing Into the Activity: If time allows and the team needs more scaffolding, each team member can be given 90 seconds to write his or her thoughts and responses to the prompt. Team members can then share with a partner. This strategy may be useful

A. if the team is reluctant to share openly,

B. if there have been past toxic behaviors,

C. if the team is still in basic formation stages, and

D. if some of the team members were not present during an important Activity preceding the current one.

Extending the Activity: After the initial prompt, the facilitator can have the team members respond to the additional prompts in the Activity. Be advised that

- these topics will likely bring out a great deal of personal background and vision from team members,
- some Activities are better suited for an experienced team, and
- discussions of certain topics with an unprepared team can sometimes do more damage than good.

Monitoring: Conversations must be carefully monitored by the facilitator to ensure that the team doesn't get into a finger-pointing cycle. The purpose of the conversation should be to illustrate and discuss how the topic at hand can benefit a team. Monitor team members carefully for feeling, tone, and sense of connection.

Participation: It is critical that the facilitator ensure that all team members share and participate. The goal of the Activities is to get team members to talk about their values on learning. The only wrong way to do the Activities is to allow members to not share. If this is the case, the facilitator or leader will have to have a critical conversation with the individual about the purpose and expectations of the team.

COMPONENTS OF TEAM ACTIVITIES

Participants: Each Activity is designed either for teams or for just the leader. Teams write out responses, share with a partner, and share with the larger group. In activities for leaders only, the leader will use the prompts for self-reflection and then write out his or her responses.

Conversation Level: Beginning, high, and so on; some activities are more successful when initiated after other Activities; more advanced Activities require advanced levels of team growth and cohesion.

Groundwork: Some Activities require prior diagnostics to be completed, in addition to the Quick-Start Diagnostic at the beginning of the book.

Purpose: Each Activity has its own purpose. It is the leader's responsibility to be aware of the purpose and to assess whether the team is ready for a particular Activity.

Goal: Each Activity has a desired goal or outcome that should be reached as a result of the conversation. Many times the goal is for the team to come to a shared understanding.

Notes for Future Use: Once the Activity is over, the facilitator should use the notes of the recorder to make his or her own notes on the efficacy of each Activity and the growth the facilitator has witnessed on the part of team members. Take note of team members who struggle more than others on a particular topic. Some people are reluctant to share when they feel that team members are not meeting certain standards.

Primary Focus Conversation: Use the initial Activity prompt as the primary focus of conversation for the team. Have each member take 30 seconds to think of a response. Then, have each member share. Have a timekeeper monitor the time. Suggested length is no more than 15 minutes.

Continue the Conversation, Additional Prompts: Use the additional prompts as follow-up questions to the Primary Focus Conversation prompt. Have each member take 30 seconds to think of a response. Then, have each member share. Have a timekeeper monitor the time. Suggested length is no more than 15 minutes per prompt.

Deeper Dives: Leaders are advised to read the entire chapter and explore the prompts as "pre-work" with your team before arriving at the Deeper Dives. The Primary Focus Conversation and Continue the Conversation prompts allow teams to develop some common conversation and thoughts before navigating deeper waters. Note: Only some chapters contain Deeper Dives as these are designed for more experienced teams. It is not advised to use any Deeper Dives with a novice or emerging team until the "pre-work" has been accomplished.

In the School: Most Activities will conclude with a very brief example of how that particular Activity was used in a real school.

PART I

Examination and Identification of the Problem

Learning
Leadership

1

INTRODUCTORY CONTENT: USE PRIOR TO ANY APPLICATION ACTIVITY IN THIS CHAPTER

LEADERS AND TEAMS

It takes leaders and it takes a team. No one can go it alone. Remember the truism: If you are the leader and you look back and no one is following, you're not leading. It takes a leader and a team.

So, what are we talking about? What does a leader have to bring to the team, and what does the team have to bring to the leader? The goal in all that we discuss is for improved student learning. Whatever we do, whatever plans we make, whatever team dynamics we tinker with, the result must be improved student learning. Otherwise, what would be the point? Let's be clear on what we're trying to accomplish.

> 🔑 **Key Thought**
>
> Whatever we do, whatever plans we make, whatever team dynamics we tinker with, the result must be improved student learning.

There are two kinds of leaders. There are instructional leaders and transformational leaders. If the goal is, as described above, to have improved student learning, then the kind of leader and teams we have to have is clear. Instructional leaders are the target. Hattie (2009) found and described the effect of both kinds of leaders on school and student performance. Instructional leaders far outperformed the transformational leaders in terms of student achievement gains. Instructional leaders have their focus on a disruption-free learning climate, clear teaching objectives, and high expectations for teachers and students. Transformational leaders have their focus on inspiring staff to collaborate to overcome challenges and reach goals. Now, to be sure, having a climate built by a transformational leader can be very positive, but the good feelings do not translate into as high a result of student gains as do those of instructional leaders. So we have to be certain that we view one as the means and one as the end. Setting a good climate in motion is key, but reaching the place of instructional leadership is where the student learning changes and improves at a higher level. Let's get to this place.

The purpose and goal of this book is about putting the systems and processes in place that support teams to uncover, discuss, and solve the issues that sustain and improve programs, initiatives, and strategies to improve student learning. The more time, effort, and maintenance given by the team to the conversations about challenging the status quo, involving teachers in designing strategies to enhance achievement, establishing challenging goals of enhanced student achievement, and monitoring feedback about student progress from all levels, the more likely student performance is to improve (Hattie, 2009).

It takes a committed leader. It takes a committed instructional leader. It actually takes a leader who goes beyond the instructional leader to become a "learning" leader. Fullan and Quinn (2016) urge that leaders need to influence the culture and processes that support learning and working together in purposeful ways at every level of the organization if they are to produce greater learning in students. Further, Fullan and Quinn (2016) describe the problem that instructional leadership leaves principals with not enough hours in the day trying to micromanage the processes of instructional leadership. Rather, the greater source of influence that a leader can have is learning leadership. Being the learning leader creates a far more binding and vital relationship of leader to teacher. Because, after all, the instruction is important and leading instruction is crucial. But, if learning is what we seek, then taking our leadership beyond instruction to learning is the highest goal of all. Your true mission is to improve learning and be a leader of learning. Be the learning leader.

> 🗝 **Key Thought**
>
> Your true mission is to improve learning and be a leader of learning. Be the learning leader.

THE REALITIES IN THE LEADERSHIP OF LEARNING

Learning leaders and their teams—let's call them learning teams—must maintain their focus. They exist to improve learning. Fullan and Quinn (2016) explain that building professional capital in organizations to support and sustain learning leadership depends on three things: (1) human capital (quality and retention of good people), (2) social capital (quality and quantity of relationships in the organization), and (3) decisional capital (making better decisions toward better results). Learning leaders must be constantly vigilant around supporting these three forms of capital. Each one of the three has its own characteristics and importance at different times and in different places, but there is never a time that one can be excluded or overlooked. Further, learning leaders and their learning teams must have the ability and regularity to discuss and visit the implications around these three forms of capital. By talking about these issues, teams can keep the focus on the causes and effects of student learning. This means that learning leaders must constantly be aware of and have dependable evidence of the effects that all the adults are having on their students (Hattie, 2012). It is precisely from this evidence that teachers, learning teams, and learning leaders must make decisions about how they teach and what they teach.

Application Activity 1.1

Assessing Your Organizational, Team, and Personal Strengths

As a leader, it is of high importance to have all members of the team be engaged and connected to the team in the delicate phase of discussion regarding current actions, ideas to improve them, and the implementation of current or improved things, techniques, programs, or strategies. Meaning, the real power behind any discussion of school improvement is to have all members of the team be connected to the team and realize the vested interest they have in engaging in a real discussion searching for real solutions.

In simplest terms, the most granular solution or goal we seek is student learning. It is the mental transaction of learning that we seek. We do all that we do to set up environments, supports, and opportunities for students to experience learning. A major task for the learning leader and the learning team is to build professional capital across the organization by modeling learning, shaping culture, and maximizing the impact on learning (Fullan & Quinn, 2016). Indeed, we work toward and do all we can to have an entire organization (school or district) hold the view that all students can learn. Kelley and Shaw (2009) describe a shared vision or preferred state where all students can learn because the environment is safe and supportive, and strong communities of practice exist among the teachers. As discussed earlier, if we seek to displace the practices of the old with a newly desired set of practices to improve learning, then it will take teams of teachers supporting each other to best install and sustain these practices. It will also take the support of the learning leader and learning team.

🔑 **Key Thought**

If we seek to displace the practices of the old with a newly desired set of practices to improve learning, then it will take teams of teachers supporting each other to best install and sustain these practices. It will also take the support of the learning leader and learning team.

We seek the transaction of learning for students. We can identify and understand the environments that allow for learning not only to occur but to occur at efficient levels. By knowing these things, we can then replicate the chances of learning again and again. This leaves the educators and leaders in a position to describe learning from their own personal behavioral perspective. What did we do or not do as the educators to set up the environments for the most effective learning? When elements are missing or not functioning, it gives us a direction to adjust and correct to give learning the best chance to occur in our classrooms, schools, and districts. It is the school leaders (learning leader and learning teams) who are the ones to promote challenging goals, and establish safe environments for teachers to critique, question, and support each other to reach these goals that have the most effect on student outcomes (Hattie, 2009).

Application Activity 1.1

Assessing Your Organizational, Team, and Personal Strengths

Participants: Teams

Conversation Level: This is great for teams that are just emerging. However, it is also appropriate for team members of all experience and skill levels.

Purpose: This Activity is designed to build trust. This Activity is meant to give team members the opportunity to tap into their values regarding education. The belief is that every team member has personal reasons regarding their purpose and the reason they do the work they do. This conversation is aimed at giving everyone a chance to share the deep inner reasons that keep them coming back day after day.

Goal: The goal of this Activity is to get team members to talk about their values of learning. The only wrong way to do this Activity is to allow a member to not share. If this is the case, the facilitator or leader will have to have a critical conversation with this individual about his or her purpose and expectation with the team.

Notes for Future Use: Keep notes on the efficacy of this Activity and the growth seen by team members.

Primary Focus Conversation

What student learning successes can you identify in your school?

What teacher actions have led to the student learning successes?

How is success celebrated?

(Continued)

(Continued)

Continue the Conversation (Additional Prompt)

1. What systems of monitoring and assessment are currently in place? Do they work? Do they work for every program? Why or why not?

Notes

IN THE SCHOOL

▶ *Madison Elementary School—The principal used this conversation with her Third-Grade Team, which had three of the five members of the team new to this grade level this school year. Her rationale was to bring out conversation about what is going well at the school and what strengths can be built on.*

Application Activity 1.2

Effective Learning Leaders

The difference makers between capable leaders and great leaders do not often start out as huge differences—meaning, at the initial stages of problem identification or solution implementation, there is not a wide gap in performance or skill between capable leaders and great leaders. But, the choices and foundations put in place at the very beginning of problem solving and their tenure make the difference. One of the most important things that great leaders do is they are always investing in strengths (Rath & Conchie, 2008). Long before a problem arises or appears on the horizon, great and effective leaders invest in their team. They invest in strengths. They find the things people do well and they build them up to be able to perform as often as possible in their strength area.

Another key area found in great and effective leaders is that they are constantly vigilant about surrounding themselves with the right people to maximize their team (Rath & Conchie, 2008). Notice what this implies. Effective leaders are those who invest in the strengths of those around them, and they constantly examine who they have on their team. But, take note: Leaders should not go it alone. Leaders don't become great leaders because they do it all themselves. Leaders also know that by definition if you turn around to see who is following you and no one is there, you're not a leader. Involving others and making those around you great is what makes great leaders.

> **Key Thought**
>
> Leaders also know that by definition if you turn around to see who is following you and no one is there, you're not a leader.

Rath and Conchie (2008) go on to explain that effective leaders are also the ones who understand their followers' needs. This idea completes the trifecta. First, work from your team's strengths. Second, be sure the right people are on the team and are positioned properly. Finally, focus on and be mindful of the team's needs. Put people in the right position and give them the right tools. Seems simple, doesn't it? But, the details and complications of an organization can cloud the things that actually happen. It takes the great leader to effectively filter the input and feedback to know what is really going on to provide the best support possible to the team.

Application Activity 1.2

Effective Learning Leaders

Participant: Leader. Use the prompts below as the primary focus self-reflection. Make note of your responses.

Primary Focus Reflection

How well do you know and understand your team members' needs?

How do you know?

(Continued)

(Continued)

Continue the Reflection (Additional Prompts)

1. What systems or processes are in place to monitor the makeup of your teams?

2. How is team chemistry used as a factor of who should be placed on which team?

3. How do you, the leader, know and invest in team member strengths?

Notes

Application Activity 1.3

Strong Learning Teams Exhibit Common Characteristics

One thing we can take from the previous activities is that leaders can't do it by themselves. It takes a team. It takes a team that functions, discusses, wrestles with situations, debates, measures, and monitors. Leaders must have a learning team, to monitor, guide, provide direction, and lend support. This learning team is there to identify and remove barriers to change, to influence and support the team's work at crucial moments, and to provide counsel and advice (Hattie, 2012).

Teams that function well have common characteristics. Hattie (2012) describes these characteristics as eight key mind frames. They are:

Eight Key Mind Frames of Teams That Function Well

1. Teachers/leaders believe that their fundamental task is to evaluate the effect of their teaching on students' learning and achievement.

2. Teachers/leaders believe that success and failure in student learning is about what they, as teachers or leaders, did or did not do.... We are change agents!

3. Teachers/leaders want to talk more about the learning than the teaching.

4. Teachers/leaders see assessment as feedback of their impact.

5. Teachers/leaders engage in dialogue not monologue.

6. Teachers/leaders enjoy the challenge and never retreat to "doing their best."

7. Teachers/leaders believe that it is their role to develop positive relationships in classrooms/staffrooms.

8. Teachers/leaders inform all about the language of learning.

Take a moment and reflect on the above list. Imagine your current organization. What if every teacher and every team had these eight mind frames present and in action at all times? What differences would you expect to see? What changes would you see in the use of assessment? Teaching? Learning? How would the school change?

Strong teams refer to these eight mind frames as an overarching guide, a reminder of what we should believe in and drive our action toward.

Strong teams focus on results. Having a purpose and goal that is greater than the individual parts is how strong teams survive and find success. When a higher purpose such as the eight mind frames are the discussion, focus, and goal, then keeping things in perspective is easier. Conflict is then seen as part of the process but not personal. Strong teams prioritize what's best for the organization and then move forward. Again, they find what is the thing to do for the entire organization.

Remember, strong teams clearly recognize that all the good ideas in the world won't change anything unless the solutions are implemented and sustained. Hattie (2012) reminds us that many good ideas fail due to low levels of degree of implementation, fidelity, or dosage. It takes a leader and a team to overcome the natural entropic inertia that exists in organizations. It takes sustained focus to build and sustain momentum. It takes routines and consistency to make the changes stick.

Application Activity 1.3

Strong Learning Teams Exhibit Common Characteristics

Participants: Teams

Conversation Level: This is great for teams that are just emerging. However, it is also appropriate for team members of all experience and skill levels.

(Continued)

(Continued)

Purpose: The purpose of this conversation is for team members to discuss the readiness of the team to engage in constructive conflict. Further, the conversation is meant to explore the basic functions of the team in being able to prioritize work well. Very often teams do neither well, or only one of the two. It is critical that all team members have the opportunity to learn of the importance of conflict and also how prioritizing can keep a team on track and moving in simple, understandable directions. Be advised that these topics will likely bring out a great deal of personal background from team members. Don't be alarmed that the sharing becomes personal and cathartic in nature. The most important thing to note is that the team members have these feelings and experiences inside them already. This process simply acknowledges in front of the team that a greater level of vigilance is needed to keep people connected and valued.

Activity Suggestions: Have team members share more deeply about their experiences with conflict that was productive and when conflict was not productive. Be advised, however, that for an emerging team with little common experience, this topic can be very risky. Although it is not a negative in and of itself for the team to share about conflict that didn't work out well, it could lead people into a state of "unearthing" the past. Traveling back in time simply to air out negative past hurts is not the point of this exercise. The point of this conversation is to recognize that conflict is necessary in a team, but it can't be so pervasive or negative that it swamps the boat. The same is true for asking for more discussion about prioritization. Most teams will not have a problem recognizing that they, their school, or their department often take on too much without narrowing the focus to the three to five things that would make the most difference.

Goal: The goal of this Activity is to get team members to talk about their values of learning.

Notes for Future Use: Keep notes on the efficacy of this Activity and the growth seen by team members.

Primary Focus Conversation

How does the team maintain prime focus on student learning and the effect that decisions have on improving student learning?

Continue the Conversation (Additional Prompts)

1. How would you assess your team in these areas:
   a. Do the learning teams dialogue about impact they have on student learning?
   b. Is the team focused on results?
   c. Do learning teams talk more about learning than they do teaching?

Notes

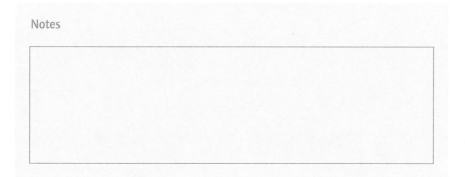

IN THE SCHOOL

▶ *Washington High School—The principal used this conversation with her Math Department Team. The purpose was to help the team reflect on the ripple effect that decisions about instructional choices can have on student learning. She wanted them to connect how much control they truly have over the results and depth of learning in their classes.*

CONCLUSION

Great leaders build and use teams. Teams allow leaders to focus on institutional goals. Teams allow for discussions of conflict, support, and direction without getting personal. Great leaders use teams to move through and solve problems. This book is not about finding problems. We can all understand that problems will occur and/or find you whether you are ready or not. This book is about being able to successfully organize and lead through the process of solving problems by using the collective strength of teams.

A Problem Worth Solving and the Ideas to Solve It (the Filters)

2

Using This Chapter

This chapter is for leaders and teams who are recognizing that there are large-scale systemic problems or issues connected to their team, school, or district. This may be that a team has come to a conclusion that a program or service is not yielding the expected results and a discussion needs to be held. This chapter helps leaders and teams open the conversation to talk about long-term change. Often these conversations are delicate and political. Involving teams is a very wise way to talk about complicated and multifaceted issues without offending or alienating people who may be very involved in the current program.

If your team or team dynamics is not currently in this place of problem identification or long-term change examination, then this chapter may not be the best use of your team's time.

It is highly recommended that readers using this chapter read the entire chapter first before using one of the Application Activities. This will give a background and perspective on the content and potential needs of the team.

INTRODUCTION

So, you have a problem. Or, so you've found a problem. Either way, this is not a surprise. Being in education brings with it an understanding that problems and challenges are all around us. They arrive, shift, and change in the blink of an eye. What wasn't a problem 20 minutes ago suddenly becomes the mountain of all mountains.

As described in Chapter 1, having or discovering a problem does not earn you a medal. Every district, every school, and every leader has problems swirling around them. It's putting the wheels in motion to handle and solve the problem that makes the difference between average organizations, good organizations, and great organizations. Some key pieces were described in Chapter 1 to simply get in the game—things such as having a learning team, knowing what team dynamics can do to build or destroy a team, knowing what our true center is (student learning), understanding that change comes with any shift in problem solving, and the importance of the learning leader in making all the difference in how problems are handled. Even thinking about how problems are talked about and discussed is critical. Understanding that conflict is not inherently bad but simply a byproduct of working through change is crucial. Conflict must be dealt with in a productive and meaningful way.

This chapter isn't about how not to have problems. Because, as we've already seen, and as you already know, problems happen no matter what. It's what you do next that counts.

IDEAS ARE FRAGILE—IDEAS ARE DELICATE

Once a problem is defined and understood, things start to happen. Now, either you start moving toward a systematic way of handling the problem or you start down a path of wasting time and missing the mark. It's this moment that matters most. You worked hard to come to understand that a problem is occurring. It is a critical point to share that the use of the word "problem" does not intend to cast a shadow or indictment on anyone. It is simply to use the word to identify something that can improve or be tightened up. Now, we shift our attention to take some time to understand how to solve the identified problem.

Once a problem is understood to be part of your organization, the first temptation is to have ideas to solve it. This is, of course, the natural reflex. But remember, solving a problem for a district or a school can be very complicated. There are many moving parts. The system is vast, and the ripple effects can be unpredictable and unwieldy. You may unwittingly solve one problem only to create 10 more. This is not the goal.

So, let's first look at how ideas are generated as possible solutions to problems. Ideas are fragile. You never know which ideas will have staying power and which ones will be scrapped. Because of that, it is critical to handle ideas gently and systematically. Know that an idea can be killed by a reaction or lack of reaction. Ideas can be blown up by sarcasm or tone of voice. Because of that, remember, you don't know when a great idea will arrive or who will have it. Knowing how to properly handle ideas in their infant stages is a prime responsibility of the leader.

> ### Key Thought
>
> You don't know when a great idea will arrive or who will have it. Knowing how to properly handle ideas in their infant stages is a prime responsibility of the leader.

Having ideas, especially for a group or organizational setting, is not easy. It is a leap of faith to share an idea, and if the setting and context are not safe and supportive, it will cause shut-down—not just in the current setting but for any future sessions as well. Ideas bring change. Change can be hard. Change brings resistance. There has to be a safe landing place for ideas even if they get discarded. Because you never know when a good one will arrive. You can't afford to shut anyone down. Even if the idea rocks the establishment, what if it's the one you've been waiting for? You can't afford to miss it.

THE FOSBURY FLOP, SKI JUMPING, AND NEWTON

Ideas are often met with a range of reaction, from excitement to dismissal to dismay to ridicule and even anger. Ideas, though usually well-meaning, bring with them the possibility of change. Change brings out interesting emotions and reactions from others. This is especially true when the idea disrupts their world. Ideas carry the power of rearranging the status quo. Very often others are not ready for the world they know to be reorganized. This brings out fears and apprehension.

Consider the track and field event the high jump. In the 1968 Summer Olympics, Dick Fosbury had an idea. He had been studying the sport and had been looking for a new way to do the high jump (Haren, 2006). He wanted to use what was known and push beyond the existing knowledge and custom of how the sport was done. The idea that Fosbury had was to run toward the high jump bar and then make one fundamental change. Instead of approaching the bar and diving over it face pointed toward the ground he had the idea of leaping over the bar with his face pointed toward the sky. The result of the jump has the athlete "flopping" onto the mat in a rather ungraceful-looking movement. The physics of this idea results in the athlete achieving a far higher leap because of the way the human back bends. Fosbury's idea won him a gold medal. It also forever changed the sport of high jump. But, it was not met with open arms. There were many who were upset and distraught at the idea of changing the custom of the sport. It was not a violation of the rules, but it did violate the custom. Despite the upset, with time, the entire sport changed. Now, no high jump athlete would ever think of doing the high jump any other way.

A similar process was experienced in the sport of ski jumping. Swedish ski jumper Jan Boklov studied and discovered that keeping the skis parallel and together when jumping might not be the best procedure (Haren, 2006). Boklov instead began to hold his skis at an angle. He greatly increased his distances. This change, though simple to understand now, was not met with great enthusiasm. But, by better harnessing the physics of air resistance, Boklov was able to split through the air and hang there for a longer period of time. And, of course, in an Olympic competition mere fractions of a second can be the difference between a medal and disappointment. In fact, Boklov's idea has forever changed the sport of ski jumping.

Isaac Newton, born in 1642, was the right person in the right place at the right time. Newton was able to take the ideas of those who came before and then rid his mind of traditional prejudices to see the universe in a new way. Newton was a very gifted mathematician who was able to invent new mathematics to solve the problems he set for himself. Newton invented the integral and differential calculus. No other invention is more prized in science than integral and differential calculus. The ideas of Gilbert plus Galileo plus Kepler plus Descartes add up to Newtonian mechanics (Van Doren, 1991). For example, you recall one of Newton's Laws: That every body continues in its state of rest or motion in a straight line unless it is compelled to change by a force placed upon it. Consider Newton's First Law of Motion, among his other amazing discoveries and explanations. Think about the ideas that must have come to his mind. Newton did not enter his work as a blank slate. He came prepared. He had spent a great deal of time understanding the science of the day. He had studied the mathematics and understood the limits of thought that had come before him. He didn't have to plow the ground that those before him had already done. Newton understood Gilbert, Galileo, Kepler, and Descartes. There was no need to restate their ideas. Instead, Newton could apply his skills to the content already brought to the table by these previous scientists and mathematicians. Newton was prepared. Newton knew how to use the tools and ideas. He pulled them together in a combination that no one previously had ever done. And, once he had the combination, he had the skill, intellect, and background to solve his own mathematical equations.

The progressive story that leads to Newton is instructive for us. Notice, Newton did not spend his time solving problems that had already been solved. He studied the earlier works to solidify his own education, but he didn't simply take the work of Descartes and Kepler and restate it. He combined things and applied things in a new order. He broke new ground. He personalized it.

Application Activity 2.1

Treating Ideas in a Learning Organization

So, as we set out to solve a problem in our school or district, consider Newton. Step One: Be sure you know all there is to know about the problem you are attempting to solve. If you have a reading comprehension issue in your school, then spend time becoming expert in reading comprehension. You won't have a Newtonian breakthrough if you don't spend the time becoming expert. Step Two: Free your mind of all existing constraints. If no constraints existed to solve your reading comprehension issue, what would you do? Seek out only the best information, programs, and ideas to combine together. Don't limit your thinking. Then, Step Three: Creatively apply your conclusions and ideas in the ways that you know will work best for your school or district. The applications and implementations of others in their schools will not transfer exactly in your environment. You must understand the peculiarities of your organization to get the most success possible and strategize in the most effective way. You solve your problem by thinking like Newton—stand on the shoulders of those who have come before you. Finally, Step Four: Monitor, measure, and analyze your idea in action. Be critical to describe growth (or lack of) in as precise a set of language as possible.

Key Thought

Problem Solving in Four Steps

Step One: Be sure you know all there is to know about the problem you are attempting to solve.

Step Two: Free your mind of all existing constraints.

Step Three: Creatively apply your conclusions and ideas in the ways that you know will work best for your school or district.

Step Four: Monitor, measure, and analyze your idea in action.

To put it another way, having ideas to solve a problem or situation requires some preparation in the arena that generated the problem. Fosbury was in the sport of high jump. He knew a great deal about it and combined it with a competitive fire. Boklov was the same. He was a ski jumper. He was intimately involved in the sport. He was immersed in it constantly. Newton understood physics and mathematics. You get the pattern.

Consider a chef. A chef does not simply become better at the culinary arts by reading recipes and cookbooks. A chef becomes better by having a solid background in culinary foundations and then combining it with practice in the kitchen to explore new ideas and combinations. In other words, it takes theory combined with practice. Rarely if ever do ideas come to the untrained or unprepared mind. Consider Isaac Newton, arguably one of the most important mathematical and scientific thinkers of all time. How did Newton come to the ideas of gravity and motion and describe them mathematically? He discovered and explained these things by thinking about them continuously. Meaning, you first have to be in the field, be immersed in it, and then train yourself to continually come up with new ideas to impact the learning in your organization.

Application Activity 2.1

Treating Ideas in a Learning Organization

Participants: Teams

Conversation Level: This is great for teams that are just emerging. However, it is also appropriate for team members of all experience and skill levels.

Purpose: This Activity is designed to build trust. This Activity is meant to give team members the opportunity to tap into their values regarding education and how the organization, as a vehicle, can support this. More important, team members have ideas all the time on how to improve the organization and their craft. What processes or systems exist to support ideas to explore them for viability? That is the purpose of this question.

Possible Topic Considerations: This Activity is designed to open up the group to trust and basic teamwork by sharing their views on the organization and how the

(Continued)

(Continued)

organization supports ideas and attempts to solve or better things. If groundwork and foundation haven't been established, this could be a very disjointed conversation for the team. It is advised to do the teamwork content in Chapter 1 before diving into this conversation.

Goal: The goal of this Activity is to get team members to talk about their views of the organization and how ideas are valued and treated.

Notes for Future Use: Keep notes on the efficacy of this Activity and the growth seen by team members. Leaders should also take careful notes on the discussions from the team about how ideas are handled. Consideration should be given to the discoveries that are shared.

Primary Focus Conversation

How should ideas and thoughts be treated in a "learning organization"?

Continue the Conversation (Additional Prompts)

1. What ideas came before Newton, Fosbury, and Boklov that led to them "putting it all together"?

2. How is this progression of thought an important parallel for your current organization?

3. Why must the people on the learning team be educated and expert in the task at hand before attempting to solve the targeted problem?

Notes

IN THE SCHOOL

▶ *Madison Elementary School—The principal used this conversation with her grade-level teams. Her rationale was to get the teams to discuss openly how ideas surface in the school and that ideas are fine but they must be studied before being used or committed to.*

Application Activity 2.2

Ideas That Don't Work: Part of the Process

One crucial concept to connect to is that every idea generated brings no expectation that it be viable. Just because you have an idea doesn't mean it's the right thing, best time, correct solution, or predictor of the future. Thomas Edison is a good example of that. He carried out 9,000 experiments before producing the most suitable light bulb. He performed more than 50,000 experiments to get to the storage battery. Those represent thousands of ideas that came and went. It's okay to have ideas. It's okay to have ideas that don't work. It's all part of the process.

🔑 **Key Thought**

One crucial concept to connect to is that every idea generated brings no expectation that it be viable.

Don't get the wrong impression. Questioning things, although often viewed as negative (boat-rockers, pot-stirrers), is not inherently negative. Questioning, if used properly, ensures that we do things right for the right reasons. Have questions. Have ideas.

Having Ideas

An idea, by definition, is a thought or suggestion toward a possible direction or action. Some people are capable of having many ideas. Some people struggle to come up with a few. Neither scenario is bad nor good. It just is. What is most important is to recognize that people who have many ideas will often require the freedom to toss most of them out. But, recognize that some of their ideas will be brilliant. So, how do you sift through the many to get to the few brilliant ideas? Or, on the other side, how does a person with few ideas get recognized if others in the group keep bringing ideas by the bushel? And in that scenario, what if a great idea is missed because someone felt crowded out?

Think about how ideas come about. Most often people do not get good ideas while in groups (Haren, 2006). Nor do good ideas often come on demand. The brain has to be able to ponder, percolate, and marinate. The conscious mind has to have its chance to talk, think, and discuss the situation and needs. But, the unconscious mind needs its chance, too. This means it is critical for a leader to understand that ideas (at least good ones) will not likely arrive in one sitting on an appointed Tuesday during your regular staff meeting. In fact, it is most likely that you have little chance of getting a good idea out of this setting at all. Set the stage and define the problem in one meeting then give people a week and check back. Having time to think, sleep, drive, eat lunch, and other routine tasks lets the conscious mind stay occupied in routine matters so the unconscious can get some work done. The point of it all is to allow some creativity to enter the scene. Creativity is using the imagination or original ideas to create something new or innovative. This is what we seek—creative and viable new ideas that will have greater impact on the learning. These are what will make the difference in classrooms, schools, districts, and in students' lives.

You can have all the ideas you want, but if they don't advance your mission and vision for learning and the school, then what good will they do? Further, if you are the only one in the school having the ideas, how likely are others to understand, support, and find excitement in your idea? Moreover, what if, heaven forbid, you happen to have the wrong idea? So how do we match the right people, with the right timing, with the right ideas? Anything short of this will likely result in wasted time, money, and effort. And that means the school stays stuck in its current trajectory.

> ### Key Thought
>
> You can have all the ideas you want, but if they don't advance your mission and vision for learning and the school, then what good will they do?

Application Activity 2.2

Some Ideas Don't Work: That's Okay, It's Part of the Process

Participants: Teams

Conversation Level: This is great for teams that are just emerging. However, it is also appropriate for team members of all experience and skill levels.

Purpose: This Activity is designed to extend trust and begin to make the connection that once there is trust and common direction, then the team can begin to talk about improvements. This Activity is meant to give team members the opportunity to tap into their experience regarding how the organization thinks about the ideas that can impact learning. More important, team members have ideas all the time on how to improve the organization and their craft. What processes or systems exist to support ideas to explore them for viability?

Possible Topic Considerations: This Activity is designed to open up the group to discuss how ideas to improve the organization are generated by sharing their views on the organization and how the organization supports ideas and attempts to solve or better things. If groundwork and foundation hasn't been established, this could be a very disjointed conversation for the team. It is advised to do the teamwork in Chapter 1 before diving into this conversation.

Goal: The goal of this Activity is to get team members to talk about their views of the organization and how ideas are valued and treated. It is imperative that all team members engage and participate.

Notes for Future Use: Keep notes on the efficacy of this Activity and the growth seen by team members. Leaders should also take careful notes on the discussions from the team about how ideas are handled. Consideration should be given to the discoveries that are shared.

Primary Focus Conversation

How do ideas that can impact learning come about in your school or district?

Continue the Conversation (Additional Prompts)

1. Are all stakeholders "allowed" to have ideas?

2. Are they given equal weight?

3. How are less than good ideas handled?

4. Are experts included in the thinking and constructing of the problem so that the ideas generated will solve the problem?

Notes

IN THE SCHOOL

▶ *Washington High School—The principal used this conversation with her Department Chair Team to explore how ideas for school improvement come forward and who is "allowed" to have ideas.*

Application Activity 2.3

It Takes Other People Sooner or Later

Now, don't panic. No one is asking you to put pressure on yourself to be the next Isaac Newton. That's not what this book is about. This chapter is about the ideas we have to solve our educational and learning problems. Having the ideas is the starting place, but then the ideas lead to solutions and solutions lead to implementation. Although this is simplified and there are steps to assist in this process, this is the basic structure.

The next thought that should arrive to you right about now is that you are very likely not a "one-woman/man show." You have others around you. They are important players. You can't set sail across the educational ocean without at least a couple other passengers and crew getting pulled into your boat. That said, you will have to describe to these passengers sooner or later where you are headed and why you're going there. It will take a learning team to get where you are going.

In fact, most ideas that move organizations forward are not the result of tremendous creative thought but rather of masterful stewardship (Belsky, 2010). Someone has to grow the idea. Someone has to nurture and sustain the idea. It is how you use what you have that makes the difference.

Making ideas happen is a combination of (1) having the idea, (2) the surrounding organization and execution, (3) the forces of community, and (4) the learning capacity to support the idea (Belsky, 2010). Of course, there are many details to describe inside these four concepts. But, it is instructive to note that organizations have to grapple with these four issues to get ideas to "happen." Even though Newton was a "one-man band," he still grappled with each of these four concepts to get his ideas and discoveries out to others beyond himself.

The organization is the guiding force of productivity (Belsky, 2010). To get your idea to happen there must be a process. In other words, just like Newton, who could invent his own mathematics to solve the problems they came up with, so it is with you and your organization. The leader must have a process designed to frame and provide a border for the work that goes on with the ideas generated to solve a targeted problem. If this isn't done, the organization will struggle and get lost on its path.

> ### 🔑 Key Thought
>
> The leader must have a process designed to frame and provide a border for the work that goes on with the ideas generated to solve a targeted problem.

Application Activity 2.3

It Takes Other People Sooner or Later

Participants: Teams

Conversation Level: This is great for teams that are just emerging. However, it is also appropriate for team members of all experience and skill levels.

Purpose: This Activity is designed to extend the previous work on trust and basic team building as well as ideas to now confront the past and challenges the organization has faced in this arena. This Activity is meant to give team members the opportunity to tap into their experience regarding how the organization has handled the ideas in the past that could impact learning.

Possible Topic Considerations: This Activity is designed to open up the group to discuss how ideas to improve the organization are generated and have been generated in the past. This topic can go to a toxic place by uncovering past mistakes or oversights. The facilitator must be prepared to steer the conversation away from a pure vent session by reminding the group to think objectively about how ideas were handled. If groundwork and foundation hasn't been established, this could be a very disjointed or even negative conversation for the team. It is advised to do the teamwork in Chapter 1 and earlier in Chapter 2 before diving into this conversation.

Goal: The goal of this Activity is to get team members to talk about their views of the organization and how ideas are valued and treated.

Notes for Future Use: Keep notes on the efficacy of this Activity and the growth seen by team members. Leaders should also take careful notes on the discussions from the team about how ideas are handled and how they have been handled in the past. Consideration should be given to the discoveries that are shared.

(Continued)

(Continued)

Primary Focus Conversation

What challenges has your organization had in the past with generating ideas or solving problems?

Continue the Conversation (Additional Prompts)

1. What processes have been evident previously in the organization to support solving a problem?

2. How does the organization currently involve a cross section of people to be part of an idea or problem-solving session?

Notes

IN THE SCHOOL

▶ *Jefferson Middle School—The principal used this reflection with his Core Math, English, Social Studies, and Science teams. He wanted them to reflect on past situations where ideas and problem solving may not have delivered all that they could have and how they can be improved.*

Application Activity 2.4

Who and What You Have Around You

Why is having ideas so important? Why should your organization have a system to handle ideas? Well, consider this question: How often does your organization stop to step back and examine how you do what you do? If you do, one of the products of this self-examination will certainly be ideas of how things can improve. How we handle these ideas will go a long way to define how the organization accelerates forward or remains stuck and stagnant.

Why would it be an important activity to stop and consider your own performance? Glei (2013) shares that when she asks a great team when was the last time they had a meeting to discuss how they work, she usually gets a null response. Sports teams have huddles to be sure they know how to run the next play. How often do your team members huddle just to talk about how they do things? If this reflection doesn't happen, then how can a leader really know who and what you have around you? Take a step back, and take stock of how improvements can be made to the system.

> ### 🔑 Key Thought
>
> How often do your team members huddle just to talk about how they do things? If this reflection doesn't happen, then how can a leader really know who and what you have around you?

Think of your work flow, especially when it comes to discussing long-range programs and plans. Have bad habits crept in over time that keep the team working at the mercy of the habits and surroundings? Has each member of the team audited the way they work and their responsibility of fixing it? Does your team, school, or district have a culture where teams should step back at least once or twice a year, not to look at *what* they are doing but instead look at *how* they do it? What benefit would each team member gain by doing this? How would the team benefit if this were a habit? What if individual team members were given the expected time and space to do a self-audit in the same way? How would the entire organization benefit by having many self-audits looking for things that would improve how they do what they do?

Application Activity 2.4

Do You Really Know Who and What You Have Around You?

Participants: Teams

Conversation Level: It is advised to do the teamwork in Chapter 1 and the earlier work in Chapter 2 before diving into this conversation.

Purpose: This Activity is designed to extend the previous work on trust and basic team building regarding ideas to now confront the present and the challenges the organization faces in this arena. This Activity is meant to give team members

(Continued)

(Continued)

the opportunity to tap into their experience regarding how the organization has handled ideas and, more important, how we get things done. This prompt will uncover disconnects between ideas and action.

Goal: The goal of this Activity is to get team members to talk about their views of the organization and how ideas are valued and treated. More interesting, this prompt will bring out disconnects between what people perceived was the direction and the actual actions that took place. It is imperative that all team members engage and participate.

Notes for Future Use: Keep notes on the efficacy of this Activity and the growth seen by team members.

Primary Focus Conversation

Does your team support self-reflection on a regular basis to examine how things are getting done?

Continue the Conversation (Additional Prompts)

1. Handling ideas is not a "throw-away" activity. Ideas require a culture of not just having them but knowing how to examine them and talk them through for viability. Does your organization have this culture? If not, what things can be done to improve or correct it?

2. Does your organization treat all ideas, on their inception, equally? Do all ideas get equal treatment? How do people react if their idea is rejected?

3. Does your team have a mechanism to sift, channel, and funnel ideas to vet them for viability?

Notes

IN THE SCHOOL

▶ Madison Elementary School—The principal used this conversation with her Leadership Team. She wanted to help the team realize that having ideas is a critical function, but realizing that some ideas may not work is even more important to understand.

DEEPER USE OF THIS CHAPTER: DEEPER DIVE

After working through the content of the chapter, you and your team can now take on some deeper conversations. Use the following prompts as catalysts to explore beliefs and values about leadership, teams, and the purpose of collective work. Leaders are advised to read the entire chapter and explore Application Activities 2.1–2.4 as "pre-work" with your team before arriving at the Deeper Dives. The Activities allow teams to develop some common conversation and thoughts before navigating the deeper water.

Answer the questions below in the context of your team, school, and/or district depending on the scope and responsibility of your task. Use the tools and reflections from this chapter to bring a greater depth to your team conversation. The questions below should be asked regarding all major initiatives, programs, or proposed solutions in your school or district.

Application Activities 2.5A–C

Deeper Dives

Participants: Teams

Conversation Level: These Activities are ideal for teams that have participated in some of the Activities from Chapter 2. These are not beginner-level discussions. Leaders should be reflective about when a team is ready to engage in these conversations. Only well-functioning and established teams should take on these topics.

Purpose: This is intended for a team that is evaluating a path of action, an idea, or a long-range decision.

Time Needed: It is hard to place a time on these Activities. The facilitator is advised to ask the group how long they wish to discuss this topic. Time will vary.

Possible Topic Considerations: The most important considerations are that there must be a basic problem that needs solving and that the team knows why. This problem, in order for it to be thought through and moved toward a solution, must be understood, and part of that understanding is for all team members to be able to articulate exactly what the problem is. It requires talking and exploration to be sure that all team members understand the problem and all the moving parts involved in the varied aspects of this problem.

(Continued)

(Continued)

Goal: The goal of these Activities is to get team members to talk about their understanding of the problem at hand. What is the team or school or organization trying to solve? Does everyone know why this problem needs solving? The goal of these Activities is that all team members have a clear understanding about the problem and why it needs solving.

Notes for Future Use: Leaders should take careful notes on the discussions from the team about the problem and the clarifications needed by the team to understand it. It will be very likely that this list of clarifications will be revisited as others are brought in to understand this problem and the directions taken. Consideration should be given to the discoveries that are shared.

Deeper Dive 2.5A—What problem needs solving? (How do you know? What has been done to verify that this is a problem worth solving?)

Deeper Dive 2.5B—Does the learning team know and understand why the problem needs solving?

Deeper Dive 2.5C—Can every member of the learning team articulate the problem?

CONCLUSION

Use the tools and reflections from this chapter to bring a greater depth to your team conversation. The questions and Application Activities in this chapter should be asked regarding any and all major initiatives, programs, or proposed solutions in your school or district.

Why Solve the Problem That Needs Solving (the Filters)

3

Using This Chapter

This chapter is for leaders and learning teams who are recognizing that there is a value and importance in knowing not just what the problem is but why the problem needs solving. Leaders and teams benefit greatly by having this common understanding and common language. This chapter will support leaders and learning teams in having the conversations about why a problem deserves to be solved.

If your team or team dynamics has already come to a firm grasp and identified tasks regarding the problem they are solving, then this chapter may not be the best use of your team's time.

It is highly recommended that readers using this chapter read the entire chapter first before using one of the Application Activities. This will give a background and perspective on the content and potential needs of the team.

INTRODUCTION

Charging off to start solving and fixing things may be a noble behavior, but it brings a serious downside. Sure, something might get done, but is it the right thing? Are there implications or ripple effects that might cause disruption in other areas of the organization? What if you solve one problem only to create three more?

These are serious reflective questions to ask. As you can imagine, the answers to these questions carry significant weight. Learning leaders and learning teams don't often take too long to make a list of things that have happened in the last couple of years that are perfect examples of setting off to fix one thing only to cause disarray in several other areas. It is a rare thing that in an organization as complicated as a school or district, a decision could truly have no ripple effect or unintended consequences. There are tentacles and shockwaves with almost every significant decision and even with many insignificant decisions.

Making a decision to act on an idea is a common task. But, even though it is common, it doesn't mean it isn't vitally important. Moreover, before we get into how we handle the processes of ideas and teams and all the related implications, let's first examine some fundamentals. Fundamentals to consider are: what a great decision looks like, why have ideas in the first place, what problem needs solving, and the role of the leader and the team in having ideas.

Application Activity 3.1

What the Result of a Great Decision Looks Like

Take a deep breath. Take a step back. Think for a moment. Think of a time when you made a decision. Think of a decision that was great. Can you describe why it was a great decision? What did you do? What was the environment like? What other people were involved? Did the decision have staying power?

The reason it is important to start things off with a reflection is that in order to get to future great decisions, it is critical to look back and know that you've done it before. You've done this. You have seen success before. You can see it again. Great decisions and great work in the past are strong clues to your future great work (Stanier, 2010). Contemplate what you are like at your best. What do great decisions and great teamwork look like? It is critical to know what great and not so great looks like. Extend your reflection to others that you can look at and study.

Scan your organization for great opportunities. Are there programs or systems that are in need of a remodel? Are there data points calling out to you that you have a performance problem somewhere? Things that distress you can also inspire you.

Getting the journey started does require some self-awareness. Consider these issues.

Do you know what your starting point is? Where are you now? Do you and your team know where you are going? Do you clearly know how you build a positive work environment (Stanier, 2010, citing Ulrich &

Ulrich, 2010)? How do you respond to setbacks? How do you manage change and all that comes with it?

Setting off on this journey of wanting to solve a problem and to have the great ideas that lead to solving the problem requires some introspection. As a leader or as a member of a team, it is crucial to examine not just what you do but how and why you do it. Further, it is critical to look back at times when decisions were made that worked. Examining great decisions for their anatomy and makeup can lead to more future great decisions.

🔑 Key Thought

As a leader or as a member of a team, it is crucial to examine not just what you do but how and why you do it.

Application Activities

Any Application Activity can be extended by bringing in more content or discussion topics. It is not recommended to take on too much in the early stages of using these tools. Teams take time to develop and gather momentum. It is best to allow teams to acclimate to the discussions and the sharing. As time and experience build, teams and leaders will find that they can handle more content in shorter blocks.

Read through the entire Activity in the main text and this support tool to prepare for the needs of the team and the room.

Application Activity 3.1

Know What the Result of a Great Decision Looks Like

Participants: Teams

Conversation Level: This Activity is not recommended for a beginning team (trust and foundational skill are needed first). But this is an excellent place to start with a team that is moving beyond the beginning stages of being a team. It is excellent for teams that are ready for a positive confidence-building conversation after basic team skills are present.

Purpose: This Activity is designed to build confidence in team members that they have made great decisions before and therefore they can do it again. This discussion builds

(Continued)

(Continued)

the members' trust and foundation that they have been there before and they can repeat their success. This discussion also helps team members understand that success breeds success, and by looking back to times when they got it right, they can be confident to repeat their success. Don't be alarmed that the sharing becomes personal and cathartic in nature. The most important thing to note is that the team members have these feelings and experiences inside them already. Be prepared to slow down as needed to allow team members to emotionally connect, share, and move on when they are ready.

Goal: The goal of this Activity is to get team members to talk about their past team successes.

Notes for Future Use: Keep notes on the efficacy of this Activity and the growth seen by team members.

Primary Focus Conversation

How might great decisions of the past assist you in future decisions?

Continue the Conversation (Additional Prompts)

1. What things or programs are most in need of attention and a remodel?

2. Have you made great decisions regarding this issue previously?

3. What made the decision great?

Notes

IN THE SCHOOL

▶ *Washington High School—The principal used this conversation with her Science Team. The team members were feeling down about recent assessment scores. The principal used this conversation to go back to previous ideas that had been successful to rebuild their confidence that they could overcome this current setback and find the ideas and solutions to break out of the present.*

Application Activity 3.2

Reasons to Have the Idea in the First Place

Looking back at previous decisions and events is important. Knowing where you've been is important. Knowing what you're trying to solve is critical. But there is one more factor at play that perhaps carries as much weight as these mentioned issues combined. Do you know and does your team know *why* you want to solve your identified problem?

Getting to the *why* requires some careful construction. One chief matter to keep in view is to be careful about what you think you know. Sinek (2009) reminds us that assumption, even based on sound research, can lead us astray. Use caution in the world of assumptions. Don't base important decisions and problem solving on assumptions.

> 🔑 **Key Thought**
>
> Don't base important decisions and problem solving on assumptions.

You can influence human behavior in only two ways: You manipulate it, or you inspire it (Sinek, 2009). This carries significant cause for reflection for any learning leader or learning team. To get people—whether on the team or outside the team—to change their behavior, you can plan only to manipulate or inspire. Obviously manipulation is a short-term solution. This is not the preferred solution set for any school or district. So, that leaves inspiration as the go-to behavior influencer. To influence people it is important to remember that people don't buy what you do, they buy why you do it (Sinek, 2009). Sinek (2009) follows this statement with a critical question: If you don't know why you do what you do, how do you expect anyone else to? This question should not be glossed over. Spend some thought and time on this. Do you know why you do what you do? Does the rest of your organization know why you do what you do? How do you know?

Once you have figured out and clearly stated why you do what you do, then you can move to the next phase. That is, how will you do what you do? There is a necessary clarity of knowing first why you do what you do, then the discipline to know how you do what you do. Finally, it must be tied together by having the consistency of knowing what you do again and again (Sinek, 2009). This "knowing" is critical not just for the learning leader and the learning team but, eventually, to communicate it regularly to the entire staff.

In order for a team or the staff to follow the leader from the *why* to the *how* to the *what*, it requires trust. Trust emerges when we have a sense that another person or organization is driven by things other than their own self-gain (Sinek, 2009). When people think you're only in it for yourself or there is a lack of communication about what you really stand for, then the possibility of trust erodes. Trust comes by communicating and demonstrating that you share values and beliefs. This communication comes by talking about the *why* and proving it with the *what* (Sinek, 2009).

Leading is all about knowing your *why* and communicating it to everyone. Leading is not the same as being the leader. Being the leader means you hold the highest rank, either by earning it or having the good fortune of navigating internal politics (Sinek, 2009). Leading is something entirely different. Leading means that others are willing to follow you. What matters most is that *what* you do and *how* you do it matches with *why* you do it (Sinek, 2009).

So, taking these ideas and coupling them with things previously discussed, we first begin to look and survey for a problem worth solving. Then, as we contemplate the ideas that might come to solve it, we have to undertake the process of matching the problem and ideas to the organization. The leaders of organizations have to be clear as to why they do what they do. The *why* should be easily understood and magnetic.

Key Thought

We first begin to look and survey for a problem worth solving. Then, as we contemplate the ideas that might come to solve it, we have to undertake the process of matching the problem and ideas to the organization.

Application Activity 3.2

Why Have the Idea in the First Place?

Participants: Teams

Conversation Level: This can be a moderate- to high-level conversation for a team. This level of discussion is not typically a good one for a newly formed team. It is best for teams to have some success working together first before exploring this topic.

Purpose: This Activity is designed to assist and remind team members that their decisions and plans must connect to the larger picture of the entire school or district.

This discussion helps a team maintain an awareness of its importance but also its place as one cog in the wheel of a much larger machine. Using this discussion provides a leader the ability to help a team have both a big-picture view as well as the small-picture detail.

Activity Suggestions: The team may uncover broad areas of past examples of confusion or lack of directional understanding. It is important for the leader and facilitator to be prepared to help a team move on and not get stuck in this place.

Goal: The goal of this Activity is to get team members to talk about their understanding of what the organization is really trying to accomplish. This discussion is meant to help members stop, think, and be sure they know why they do what they do.

Notes for Future Use: Keep notes on the efficacy of this Activity and the growth seen by team members.

Primary Focus Conversation

How will we align the problem our team is focusing on to the why of the organization?

Continue the Conversation (Additional Prompts)

1. Does the problem fundamentally shift us away from the things we do? (Is the problem causing a misalignment or distraction from our primary task?)

2. Is the *why* understood and clearly communicated from the leader to the team and to the organization?

Notes

IN THE SCHOOL

▶ *Jefferson Middle School—The principal used this reflection with his Fine Arts Team. He wanted to help team members examine their ideas in the larger context of the mission of the school. He wanted them to find a connection with the learning going on in the other departments.*

Application Activity 3.3

The Problem That Needs Solving: Clear, Concise

It is a leadership issue. It depends on the leader to initiate it. The leader must host the conversation to seek ideas to solve the identified problems. Sounds simple, doesn't it?

As a leader, especially a leader taking on the conversation of gathering ideas to solve an identified problem, it would be wise to keep some things in view to aid you along the path. It is very, very common that in today's educational landscape, which often includes significant change (standards, assessments, evaluations, finance, etc.), it really boils down to the most important things. Do you know what the most important student learning issues are? Do you know what the most significant resource issues are? Do you understand the most important local political issues? Sadly, with so much change going on, few leaders will find themselves prepared to carry out this new agenda (Hess, 2013). The skills of the old world will take you only so far in the new world. So, let's be clear on at least one skill set: how to frame an identified problem and work it toward a systemic solution and quality implementation.

First, be clear in what you are wanting. Clarity on not just what you're doing but what you think a great school system looks like is the first thing to get nailed down (Hess, 2013). Don't settle for ineptitude and excuse making—see things clearly and discuss them precisely (Hess, 2013). Describe and name problems as they are, and set precise goals to fix them. Be specific about the goals. Make them concise and measurable. Always keep the problem you are solving in mind. The goals should align to the problem. Make every conversation be about a problem and how you are solving it (Hess, 2013).

> **Key Thought**
>
> Describe and name problems as they are, and set precise goals to fix them.

How well do you think differently? Solving today's problems with yesterday's solutions will lead to mediocrity at best. Push yourself and those around you to think differently. Think beyond money as the easy fix. Think of all the things you can do before money enters the picture. There are many things that can be done, tightened up, supported, and given new life without using money.

Some critical mistakes to keep an eye on include (1) using data haphazardly and (2) translating or misapplying research simplistically. Data can tell many stories. Be very careful that you don't allow data that may have a skew or a more complicated story to dominate the conversation about action or targets. Be sure you have access to data (both formative and summative) that are tightly aligned to the problem at hand. That way the cause and effect relationship will be easily understood. Looking at research that was meant to show one thing should be carefully examined for its generalizability. Don't make a shoe fit that doesn't fit. It will only make your foot hurt, and it will damage the shoe. Don't make research fit that doesn't fit.

Measure the things that matter the most. If something can't be measured, you should examine it with a wary eye. Measure more than test scores. Be sure that you have ready access to data for the things that must be measured. Always have your metrics and measurements working for you—and not that you are working for them (Hess, 2013). Keep things in a proper perspective. It is up to the leader to set this tone.

> **🔑 Key Thought**
>
> Measure the things that matter the most. If something can't be measured, you should examine it with a wary eye.

Discovering a problem is as easy as finding an apple on an apple tree. They are all around you. What isn't easy is keeping the focus on things that can be measured. Keep the focus on clear and concise discussions and definitions about your problem. Keep a focus on gathering and examining data about your problem. These are the things that help a leader see a problem, define the problem, and open the door to have the proper ideas to solve the problem.

Application Activity 3.3

What Problem Needs Solving: Be Clear, Be Concise

Participants: Teams

Conversation Level: These conversations are for more experienced teams. Beginning teams may understand the need for data on programs, but they won't have had mutual experience on the collective success of doing it together.

(Continued)

(Continued)

Purpose: This Activity is designed to remind a team of the importance of being able to measure its progress. This conversation helps ground team members in the expectation going in that anything of value they choose to do should include a data component to track progress. This conversation is not meant to point out things a team is not doing or not doing well. The conversation is meant to reignite the purpose and direction for team members so they can measure the good things they do. This conversation is meant to spark greater energy from members, not make them feel bad or inadequate. The continuing conversations can be extended to go even deeper, not just in the current state of the team but in the future desired state as well.

Goal: The conversations are meant to help members remember the importance of data in their work. The leader or facilitator has to be careful that the team stays in a positive and energetic state of mind in this discussion. Do not allow the past to cloud the potential of the future. This can be a pivotal moment for a team. Grasping the importance of data and measurement in a program are among the most important things a team will do.

Notes for Future Use: Keep notes on the efficacy of this Activity and the growth seen by team members.

Primary Focus Conversation

How do you use data regarding your identified problem? Are they easy to gather? Are they clear and understandable when you get them?

Continue the Conversation (Additional Prompts)

1. How clear is the problem? Is it clear only to the leader? How specific and granular can you be about your problem?

2. Do you have data, research, and feedback loops established for your identified problem? How well are the three areas (data, research, and feedback loops) functioning?

Notes

IN THE SCHOOL

▶ *Washington High School—The principal used this conversation with her English Team. The team was coming up with many ideas to focus on nonfiction writing. The prompts assisted the team members not only to find data to target the problem itself but also to find a data source as they begin to work on their implementation.*

Application Activity 3.4

The Role of the Leader in Developing Ideas

Sometimes spontaneity is a good thing. Throwing a surprise birthday party. Bringing home an unexpected gift. Taking an old friend out for dinner just because it's a Thursday in May. Things like these are fun, light-hearted, and welcome surprises. Solving problems in your school or district are not the same light-hearted affairs. These things often have deep cultural roots and many layers. Snap, spontaneous ideas to solve deep problems is a recipe for confusion, disconnect, and loss of faith.

Indeed, it should be clear by now that the leader plays a crucial role in hosting the forum and conversation not only to clearly identify the problem but also to talk about the ideas that can be used to solve the targeted problem. Ideas brought forward with no clear purpose or no clear forum to discuss and vet them lead only to mental clutter. This leaves some team members feeling misunderstood or undervalued because they felt they had a good idea, but no one could wrap their head around it and it stalled. It leaves others on the team feeling like their wheels are spinning because seeing the problem is clear, but there is no sense of accomplishment that a solution will ever be found. These symptoms, and more like them, are responsibilities that lie at the feet of the leader. It isn't up to the leader to think of every solution to every problem. But, it is the responsibility of the leader to build a process and system so that the problem can be adequately discussed and the ideas that lead to solutions can also be brought forward and evaluated.

🔑 Key Thought

Ideas brought forward with no clear purpose or no clear forum to discuss and vet them lead only to mental clutter.

The leader must be the one who puts the frame around the discussion. This frame must not only suffice for discussion of the problem but also host the conversation about the ideas to solve it. In other words, the leader must place the parameters around the problem, the ideas, and the targeted solution. Having free-form ideas works only when you are alone. When matters involving a team come up, no single person can have the ideas to carry the team. Directionless brainstorm may be a fun thing to have, but it really works only when you're alone solving problems just for you. When it comes to a team, school, or district, ideas cannot be used in isolation. The ideas must have a process to connect the whole team and unify its purpose. Meaningful ideas require direction.

Key Thought

When matters involving a team come up, no single person can have the ideas to carry the team.

As a leader, bear in mind that the leadership involved in creating a frame for discussion is very much an "experience-driven" leadership skill. Leaders gain the experience of how to host these conversations and lead these teams through the experience of trial and error (Belsky, 2010). Each problem and each set of proposed ideas brings with them all new details and circumstances. Having solved problems in the past and managed the flow of ideas brings good experience, but there will always be adjustments. We must be self-aware enough to know when things and processes are working and when they are not. Then, we must take action to remedy the symptoms we observe.

The most important thing in all of this is to get in there and try. The problems won't solve themselves. The ideas, especially the good ones, won't appear and fall from the sky. These things all take proper forums and work. It's all right to be wrong. It's unknown territory and there's no way of knowing what can happen, but there's more of a chance of it's being amazing if you try (Arden, 2003). Risk is involved in all of this. But don't let risk or the fear of being wrong stop you from trying to solve something worth solving. Risks are a measure of people. People who don't take risks are trying to hold on to what they have. Take the risk to solve the problems. Take a risk to make your school better. Take a risk to talk about things that need to be talked about.

It takes awareness. It takes a leader. It takes a forum. It requires the ability to talk about the problems that most need solving. It takes a system and process to handle the incoming ideas. It takes courage to push out there and take a risk. It takes courage to absorb the energy and anxiety that can come from untangling long-standing organizational behaviors. Take the risk anyway.

Application Activity 3.4

The Role of the Leader in Developing Ideas

Participants: Teams

Conversation Level: This discussion is meant for teams that have already built a good and solid foundation in basic team functions. In order for this conversation to work with team members, they have to have a working relationship that allows for new ideas to surface and be handled in a safe and respectful manner. Asking members to think of ideas for improvement too early in their connection could lead to hurt feelings of implication that things haven't been going well and that blame should be assigned. This *must* not be allowed to happen. Leaders and facilitators should be careful as to when this topic is used.

Purpose: This Activity is designed to bring a self-reflection to team members where they introspect to think about their readiness to bring ideas to the table to solve identified issues.

Goal: The goal of this Activity is to get team members to talk about their thoughts on how ideas can be brought forward.

Notes for Future Use: Keep notes on the efficacy of this Activity and the growth seen by team members.

Primary Focus Conversation

What is the readiness level of the team to bring ideas to the table to solve the identified problems?

Continue the Conversation (Additional Prompts)

1. What readiness issues does your team have to talk about the problems that most need to be talked about?

2. What experience do you have or does the leader have in managing a team through the problem-identification phase or the idea-gathering phase?

(Continued)

(Continued)

Notes

IN THE SCHOOL

▶ *Madison Elementary School—The principal used this conversation with her Leadership Team. She wanted to help the team realize that the team has to be ready to have ideas to solve schoolwide issues. She wanted to be sure that the team understood that all members must play an active role in having and discussing ideas.*

Application Activity 3.5

Harnessing the Forces Around You

Throughout this chapter, we have discussed the basic tools of first understanding that there is a problem in need of a solution. This basic tool set also includes the realization that problems bring ideas. But, we have to have a process and leadership to properly handle the ideas. Simply having ideas may not be so difficult. But, having the right ideas at the right time and in the right place can prove to be a much more challenging task than it seems at first blush.

A key understanding in having ideas and getting the right ideas working for you is to harness the people around you. Some of the team members are better suited for certain parts of the process than others. Belsky (2010) describes these people as Dreamers, Doers, and Incrementalists. Dreamers are fun to be around, but they struggle to stay focused. Doers don't imagine as much because they are obsessively focused on execution. Doers will take any idea, start with doubt, and chip away at it until they either love the idea or hate the idea. Incrementalists play the role of both Dreamer and Doer. Incrementalists have the tendency to conceive and execute too many ideas simply because they can.

Interestingly enough, you can probably think of many of the people on your team and imagine which of the three types they are. Certainly it is easy to understand that all three types need each other to run at maximum capacity. Having a room with all one type will spin things in circles. Having two types but not the third can be deadly because groupthink can creep in. No one will be there to challenge the thinking with the other end of the continuum. The team should ideally be made up of members from all three schools of thought. This makeup allows not only for ideas to be shared and debated but also for momentum in the room to act as a catalyst to get it done (Belsky, 2010). Doers will be critical to be sure an idea can actually hit the ground and get in place. Dreamers will be busy thinking of the next great thing, while the Incrementalists will go back and forth between both sides helping momentum shift from side to side to push the process to its best product.

> **Key Thought**
>
> Doers will be critical to be sure an idea can actually hit the ground and get in place. Dreamers will be busy thinking of the next great thing, while the Incrementalists will go back and forth between both sides helping momentum shift from side to side to push the process to its best product.

Know thy team. A crucial issue is to be sure you have diversity on the team. It is a lethal mistake for a leader to build a team that is all one type or, worse still, that is made up of people just like him or her. Remember, there's already one of you. Having a room full of types just like you only increases the number of people. It does not necessarily increase the creativity or solutions.

Application Activity 3.5

Harnessing the Forces Around You

Participant: Leader. Use the prompts below as the primary focus self-reflection. Make note of your responses.

(Continued)

(Continued)

Primary Focus Reflection

How do the skills of each team member complement you? How do
you know they are different from you? What crucial ingredient
does each team member bring to the table?

Take some reflective time to assess who you have around you. Can you
identify if they are Dreamers, Doers, or Incrementalists?

What part does each team member play?

Notes

DEEPER USE OF THIS CHAPTER: DEEPER DIVES

After working through the content of the chapter, you and your team can now take on some deeper conversations. Use the following prompts as catalysts to explore beliefs and values about leadership, teams, and the purpose of collective work. Leaders are advised to read the entire chapter and explore Application Activities 3.1–3.5 as "pre-work" with your team before arriving at the Deeper Dives. The Activities allow teams to develop some common conversation and thoughts before navigating deeper waters.

Answer the questions below in the context of your team, school, and/or district depending on the scope and responsibility of your task. Use the tools and reflections from this chapter to bring a greater depth to your team conversation. The questions below should be asked regarding any and all major initiatives, programs, or proposed solutions in your school or district.

Application Activity 3.6A

Deeper Dive

Participants: Teams

Conversation Level: This Activity is ideal for use with a team that has used some of the other activities from this chapter. It is not a beginner-level discussion. Leaders and facilitators should be reflective about when a team is ready to open up this conversation.

Purpose: This Activity is designed to clarify the direction of the team. This is to assist "getting everyone on the same page." Being sure that all members can talk about where they are and where the team is going is vital for building collective efficacy.

Goal: This conversation is absolutely critical for teams to be confident that all members know what their purpose and direction is. This conversation helps teams be sure that all members are rowing in the same direction.

Notes for Future Use: Keep notes on the efficacy of this Activity and the growth seen by team members.

Deeper Dive 3.6A—Can every member of the team articulate the problem and the proposed solution(s)?

Application Activity 3.6B

Deeper Dive

Participants: Teams

Conversation Level: This is a very high-level conversation for a team. Only well-functioning and established teams should take on this topic.

Purpose: This activity is designed to let team members reflect and discuss their perceived readiness to take on an identified deep problem or situation.

Goal: The outcome is to give a team a purposeful direction and common target.

Notes for Future Use: Keep notes on the efficacy of this Activity and the growth seen by team members.

Deeper Dive 3.6B—How ready are the members and the leader to take on the solving of the problem?

Application Activity 3.6C

Deeper Dive

Participants: Teams

Conversation Level: This is a very high-level conversation for a team. Only well-functioning and established teams should take on this topic.

(Continued)

(Continued)

Purpose: This conversation is meant to let a team think about the critical aspect of who is available to work on a particular problem. This way there is consideration given to the readiness of a team and knowledge that there are truly people available to assist.

Goal: This conversation is absolutely critical for teams to be confident that all members know what their purpose and direction is. This conversation helps teams be sure that all members are rowing in the same direction.

Notes for Future Use: Keep notes on the efficacy of this Activity and the growth seen by team members.

Deeper Dive 3.6C—What resources and people are available to assist in solving the problem?

CONCLUSION

Use the tools and reflections from this chapter to bring a greater depth to your team conversation. The questions and Application Activities in this chapter should be asked regarding any and all major initiatives, programs, or proposed solutions in your school or district.

PART II

Introspection, Behaviors, Types: The *How* and *Who* to Solve Problems

How th...
Solved

that could solve th...
tion. There is on...
the team cohe...
A proce...
the "rules...
describ...
tions...
tal...

Using This Chapter

This chapter is for leaders and learning teams who are recognizing that there is a direct correlation between the mind-set and skills that team members come with and the productivity of the team. Teams and leaders who are still developing in their skill sets and understanding of teams will benefit from the content and Activities in this chapter. Some of the Activities are useful for the entire team, and some are appropriate for the leader.

If your team has already come to a firm grasp of the personal skills and team skills needed to have productive conversations and team meetings, then this chapter may not be the best use of your team's time.

It is highly recommended that readers using this chapter read the entire chapter first before using one of the Application Activities. This will give a background and perspective on the content and potential needs of the team.

INTRODUCTION

Through the earlier chapters of the book, we have looked at and discussed some of the key preliminary steps to understanding problem identification and having the ideas to solve them. These preliminary steps cannot be underestimated. It is absolutely critical that a learning team or an organization have a mechanism to identify problems and a clear way that ideas are brought forward to solve these identified problems.

But let's be clear about something. Just because you have identified a problem and even perhaps found some ideas (programs, services, strategies)

e problem, you're not quite ready to tackle the situa-
e very important structure that must be present to keep
sive and functioning: A process.

ss is a set, clearly articulated structuring device that provides
of the road" for all team members. This means that the process
es the flow of work, the involvement of the members, the expecta-
, the monitoring, and the intended targets of success. The process
es the guesswork out of what the team will do and what the targets are.
urther, the process allows everyone to have agreed-upon performance
expectations where the group members hold one another accountable.
People who don't perform are transparently known to the entire group.
This soft accountability and peer pressure is far more successful at correct-
ing behavior for the long haul than any "meet your maker" conversation
the leader may provide.

Application Activity 4.1

Importance of a Process

Having a process or system to examine problems and ideas to search for
the best path is important because it provides an overall frame for behavior and performance. The process also helps manage the flow of work one
step at a time. In other words, it is important to have "big picture" processes (an overall frame) as well as "detail" processes (work flow one step
at a time). The leader must support the creation of both.

The big-picture processes are critical because these govern how a
team comes together. These processes pieces assist in describing behavior,
how the work will flow, dates, goals, purpose, and contingency plans.
These are the big targets.

The micro-level processes are critical because these are the mechanisms where the work gets done—meaning, how ideas are actually
handled. How problems are brought to light. Micro-level processes dive
into the minutiae and specifics of every step. The who, what, when,
where, and how are all necessary steps in the micro-level processes.

Processes are a lot like a garden. The garden requires soil preparation,
fertilizer, water, sunlight, oxygen, time, and weeding. But, with the proper
and diligent inputs, the outputs can be amazing. So it is with processes to
solve problems in your organization. The processes don't invent themselves. The processes don't maintain themselves. But well-maintained
processes are the difference between organizations that make sustained,
successful progress and those that find it (or don't find it) by random
chance. And, random chance is not what leaders are paid to do.

Key Thought

Well-maintained processes are the difference between organizations that make sustained, successful progress and those that find it (or don't find it) by random chance.

Application Activity 4.1

Importance of a Process

Participants: Teams

Conversation Level: This can be a moderate- to high-level conversation for a team. This level of discussion is not typically a good one for a newly formed team. It is best for teams to have some success working together first before exploring this topic.

Purpose: The purpose of this Activity is for teams to reflect on past tasks to identify if a process was present or not. Further, this Activity is designed to reflect on behaviors in the team or leadership that supported the use of processes.

Goal: The goal of this Activity is for team members to recognize that having a process is vital and necessary. It also points out that they have been there before and they know what it feels like to drift and have no process to refocus the team.

Notes for Future Use: Take note of team members who struggle more than others when a process is failing or not present. They could be good "canaries in the coal mine" to alert the team when processes are breaking down or lacking.

Primary Focus Conversation

Describe two or three situations where there was no observable process for a team or task. What were the feelings of connection (or lack of) from the members?

Continue the Conversation (Additional Prompts)

1. Describe processes (either macro or micro) that have been successfully put in place in the organization before. What made them successful?

2. What was the end product from a situation that had no observable process? Was the product performance hindered by disconnect and ambiguity? Describe.

3. Describe the behavior of the leaders in the two question prompts above. What did they do or what did they miss that made the situations what they were?

(Continued)

(Continued)

Notes

IN THE SCHOOL

▶ *Washington High School—The principal used this conversation with her Accreditation Team. She recognized that the team did not have a collective understanding of why having visible and understandable processes keeps people connected to school improvement projects.*

Application Activity 4.2

Trust

We will now shift a gear to look at issues in a much broader scope. This is an observation of the team itself. Note for the leader: This book focuses on the team structure and dynamics. This book does not focus on the mechanics of structuring and choosing a team. Nor does this book focus on setting up the team. This book assumes that the team is constituted and has basic functioning skill.

This book looks at the tasks of the team and the broad issues of keeping the team pointed in the right direction. Basically, we will examine team dynamics through two questions: (1) Are we ready to be a team, and (2) Are we ready for heavy lifting? This is why the assumption is made that the team is already there and in functioning condition. Our focus is on getting to the outputs that will really make a difference for your school or district. To do that, let's look at some of the issues that may prevent you from getting to the ability of being a team and doing heavy lifting.

Trust—or more appropriately a lack of trust—is a major issue that will block a team from being a team. It will certainly prevent the team from doing the work that will really make a difference. Lencioni (2005) reminds us that members of great teams trust each other. What he means by trust is that members of the team have vulnerability (weaknesses, failures, mistakes, and fears). This vulnerability allows for open, honest conversation as well as an ability to understand present conditions and capacity.

For the leader, remember that trust is the foundation of teamwork (Lencioni, 2005). Trust takes time. Trust takes work. Trust takes maintenance. Trust not only requires a sense of dependability but also a sense of realistic honesty to acknowledge when things did or didn't go well. Teams will dissect the good and the bad in a way that dignity is maintained for the individual but the issue will be thoroughly examined for next steps. Trust in a basic sense means people do what they say they're going to do. Be there when you're supposed to be there. Carry the mission and vision of the team even when you are on your own.

🔑 **Key Thought**

Trust not only requires a sense of dependability but also a sense of realistic honesty to acknowledge when things did or didn't go well.

Absence of trust in a team is a major indicator of a team not operating at capacity. This must be addressed immediately. The true success you seek in your organization will not be realized if full trust is not happening or if you're not moving toward it.

Application Activity 4.2

Trust

Participant: Leader. Use the prompts below as the primary focus self-reflection. Make note of your responses.

Primary Focus Reflection

Examine your current team. Discuss the level of trust seen on the team. What are the blocks and barriers? What is necessary to build the needed trust?

(Continued)

(Continued)

Notes

Application Activity 4.3

Fear of Conflict

In the same way firefighters are trained to run into a burning building when all instincts scream to run the other way, so too must leaders. Except instead of running into the burning building, leaders must confront conflict. Notice that confronting conflict indicates that it is present in the first place. Often schools and school leaders cite lack of conflict on their teams as signs of positive performance. What it actually indicates is that team members are holding back, avoiding the real issues, and squashing their true feelings. In order to get where you really want to go, it will take some conflict.

People have to be free to disagree and debate their position. In fact, members of great teams do just that. Members of great teams passionately dialogue and debate issues that are key to the organization's success (Lencioni, 2005). This is, of course, predicated on the notion that these team members genuinely want to find the best answers, discover the truth, and make great decisions.

Conflict is not easy. Conflict brings discomfort. In advance of tackling conflict, teams must have norms that have been discussed and made clear (Lencioni, 2005). Conflict in the absence of norms brings division, anger, and hurt. Productive conflict, on the other hand, requires trust so that team members engage in unfiltered, passionate debate about issues in a nonpersonal manner. But, that said, teams should not completely avoid the occasional personal conflict. The norms and the enforcement of the norms should allow even this type of conflict to be aired out and handled. The worst thing of all is to know that conflict exists and to do nothing. The conflict won't go away. It will just go underground, certain to resurface one day more ugly than it was the day it went below the soil line.

> ### 🔑 Key Thought
>
> Productive conflict, on the other hand, requires trust so that team members engage in unfiltered, passionate debate about issues in a nonpersonal manner.

Application Activity 4.3

Fear of Conflict

Participant: Leader. Use the prompts below as the primary focus self-reflection. Make note of your responses.

Primary Focus Reflection

Reflect on the ability of the team to handle conflict. Does it happen?

Does it become personal? What are the sources of conflict?

How can people's skill with conflict be improved?

Notes

Application Activity 4.4

Commitment

First comes trust. Next comes conflict. After that comes commitment. Teams that don't have trust can never address and use conflict properly. If conflict can't be handled properly, then teams never get true and genuine buy-in about important decisions (Lencioni, 2005). Teams with trust and proper conflict are able to put all options on the table with an ability to consider them. This process shows a team that no stone has been left unturned and everything has been thought through and considered. This truly gives team members the opportunity to commit to the decision.

Commitment is not consensus. Lencioni (2005) warns not to wait for consensus. In fact, Lencioni (2005) reminds us that defying consensus is the goal. Your task is not to try and get a majority of people or a consensus to agree on where you're going. The goal really is to get people to commit to a path due to buy-in and clarity.

Clarity requires that teams avoid ambiguity and assumptions. Members of great teams can still commit to decisions they disagree with because the process was open, fair, thorough, and based on trust and conflict. Getting to clear understanding via debate and examination brings buy-in. Consensus can sometimes be a substitution for "give-in."

Application Activity 4.4

Commitment

Participants: Teams

Conversation Level: This can be a moderate- to high-level conversation for a team. This level of discussion is not typically a good one for a newly formed team. It is best for teams to have some success working together first before exploring this topic.

Purpose: The purpose of this Activity is for teams to reflect on past success and the role that commitment played. Further, teams will explore the ingredients that were present and necessary for success due to commitment.

Goal: The goal of this Activity is to let team members discuss the importance of committing to a process.

Notes for Future Use: Keep notes on the efficacy of this Activity and the growth seen by team members. Take note of team members who struggle more than others when a process is failing or not present. They could be good "canaries in the coal mine" to alert the team when processes are breaking down or lacking.

Primary Focus Conversation

What ingredients were present when success was visible due to broad commitment of the team to the process?

Continue the Conversation (Additional Prompts)

1. Discuss the differences of commitment versus consensus.

2. What ingredients were present when success was visible due to broad commitment?

Notes

IN THE SCHOOL

▶ *Jefferson Middle School—The principal used this reflection with his Leadership Team. He used these prompts because he recognized that in order for his schoolwide focus to move forward, it would require commitment and understanding from all stakeholders.*

Application Activity 4.5

Accountability

First there must be trust, conflict management, and commitment. Then comes accountability. For teams to function and actually get the hard work done that makes a lasting difference, there must be a mechanism of accountability. Teams that have trust, deal with conflict, and commit to difficult things do not hesitate to hold one another accountable to the agreed-upon decisions and standards of performance (Lencioni, 2005). Another key indicator that the team is built solidly from the ground up is that the accountability is not held primarily or solely with the leader. Peers take ownership and talk with one another about accountability and performance.

> 🔑 **Key Thought**
>
> Another key indicator that the team is built solidly from the ground up is that the accountability is not held primarily or solely with the leader.

As described earlier, developing a structure and culture with a team that leads to a system where accountability can be handled between team members because the trust, conflict, and commitment management is strong takes effort and perseverance. One of the most important indicators that a team can reach this level of performance is that the leader demonstrates a willingness to confront difficult issues along the way (Lencioni, 2005). Also, it should be noted that the best place for team members to function with this kind of accountability is during regular meetings (Lencioni, 2005). This is true because the meeting room should be where data charts and performance artifacts are present. This allows for natural discussion in a regular and systematic way of the performance trends and data. Having this discussion of performance and accountability is also best done in the meeting room because the established norms of behavior and conflict will be most readily enforced.

Application Activity 4.5

Accountability

Participants: Teams

Conversation Level: This can be a moderate- to high-level conversation for a team. This level of discussion is not typically a good one for a newly formed team. It is best for teams to have some success working together first before exploring this topic.

Purpose: This Activity is designed to help a team combine the need for process with an accountability to keep the team members connected and responsible to their direction. It is not enough for a team to commit to a process; there has to be follow-through. Building accountability allows the team members to hold each other to a commitment of productivity but also to create support for those who struggle from time to time. It is not meant to delve into why the process or accountability wasn't there. That is not productive. The leader or facilitator must be prepared to steer a team away from this.

Goal: The team members should arrive at a place where having a reasonable accountability to their process is agreed upon and able to be accomplished.

Notes for Future Use: Keep notes on the efficacy of this Activity and the growth seen by team members.

Primary Focus Conversation

What accountability systems or processes are present for the team?

Continue the Conversation (Additional Prompts)

1. What accountability systems or processes need to change?

2. How can the accountability be as omnipresent as water is to a fish?

3. How will the team arrive at this place?

Notes

IN THE SCHOOL

▶ *Washington High School—The principal used this conversation with her Social Science Team. The team members have worked for several semesters on refining their end-of-semester assessments. These conversations were used to keep the team focused on the impor- tance of accountability in both the process and the end product.*

Application Activity 4.6

Attention to Results

It should be clear as the discussion has unfolded in this section that creat- ing and maintaining these processes is like building a skyscraper. It is impossible to talk about the fancy penthouse restaurant on the 33rd floor without having a solid foundation and smart blueprints on the lower floors. So it is with building a team and team dynamic that can get things done at a high level of performance. Teams that have trust, have conflict, commit to decisions, and hold one another accountable are the most likely to set individual needs aside and focus on what's best for the team (Lencioni, 2005). It is only when teams reach this level of performance and functionality that real differences of a lasting nature will be seen in the organization.

There are some temptations and performance-killers that lurk out there in the shadows that are always present. Even after all the effort to get the team to this level where trust, conflict, commitment, and accountabil- ity are all happening, there are problems that require constant vigilance. The first problem in the shadows to be looking for is ego. Ego is the ulti- mate killer on a team (Lencioni, 2005). Ego has to be put aside, and the success of the team and organization has to come first. The second and third killers are career development and money (Lencioni, 2005). People can't be allowed to make decisions solely from a frame of reference that it will boost their career or give them a financial gain. The fourth killer is when people protect "their department" (Lencioni, 2005). There shouldn't be an ownership of this magnitude. Teams should look at pieces of the organization as tools and resources to accomplish tasks. If people and things require shuffling or rearranging to get the maximum performance from the whole team or organization, then it has to happen. There can't be blocks that slow down progress.

Great teams have the things described earlier but they also have a relentless drive to see and get results that they set out to achieve. Great teams measure themselves by progress and results. Team members must place the results above individual or departmental needs. One way to keep this focus on the team and not slipping into individual or departmental discussions is to have public sharing and clarification of their results (Lencioni, 2005). Keeping the targets and results visible provides the best mechanism for keeping a high-functioning team moving and making progress.

🔑 **Key Thought**

Great teams measure themselves by progress and results.

Application Activity 4.6

Attention to Results

Participants: Teams

Conversation Level: This can be a moderate- to high-level conversation for a team. This level of discussion is not typically a good one for a newly formed team. It is best for teams to have some success working together first before exploring this topic.

Purpose: This Activity is designed to assist a team in having conversations about results and being results oriented. Teams having this discussion should be able to talk about past experiences linked to results and the successes that came because of that focus. This discussion also pushes a team to always keep programs anchored in results.

Goal: The team should arrive at a place where having a reasonable focus on results is agreed upon and able to be accomplished.

Notes for Future Use: Keep notes on the efficacy of this Activity and the growth seen by team members.

Primary Focus Conversation

How are results used?

Continue the Conversation (Additional Prompts)

1. What will have to change to make results a constant presence?

2. How will team members get to this level?

Notes

IN THE SCHOOL

▶ *Madison Elementary School—The principal used this conversation with her Second-Grade Team. The team was not very successful in reading intervention work. The principal used these prompts to help the team members find their motivation and confidence that they can drive toward lofty goals that are results driven.*

Application Activity 4.7

Generating Ideas and Action Steps

It was important to talk about the team before we talk about handling ideas. It should be a logical connection. Talking about ideas in a nonteam setting is a leadership toxic bomb waiting to go off. How will the team be able to discuss the true problems at hand? How will the team arrive at a path to choose? How will there be any hope of actually moving forward and making progress? This is not a "which came first—the chicken or the egg" type riddle. In this case, the team comes first. Ideas to solve problems come second. Always.

Now, assuming you are on the road to getting the team built and operational, we can begin our readiness to take on ideas to solve real problems. The skill set most valued in having ideas is the ability to search for relationships between facts (Young, 2009). This skill is not innate. It can be developed and grown. The notion is that we seek ideas to solve problems in our school where we look for a new combination or a new relationship between facts, data, or observations. It is the ability to see new relationships that matters the most.

> ### 🔑 Key Thought
>
> The notion is that we seek ideas to solve problems in our school where we look for a new combination or a new relationship between facts, data, or observations. It is the ability to see new relationships that matters the most.

To get to the discussion and mental noshing needed to connect ideas to the current state requires the earlier chapters of gathering data and raw material about the problem. It also requires gathering research, possible solutions, and anything else related, both specific and general (Young, 2009). Now, the task is to look at things like a jigsaw puzzle. This is the period where patience will come into play. Having the idea and coming up with the relationship explanation will not come in one meeting. Be persistent in examining the puzzle pieces. But, don't push the process faster than the wheels can spin. Team members will need to have time. Nights of sleep. Time commuting in the car. The unconscious mind can do a tremendous amount of work when it is left alone. Stopping to specifically think is often the least productive way to get to a solution. Good ideas come because they're ready. They come because they connect the puzzle pieces to solve what you're trying to solve. The good ideas will shape and develop in a natural way. Having a team structure to meet, talk, share, argue, debate, and search is the only way to have a reasonable chance of getting all the identified needs addressed.

Another key reason to be sure the team and a process is built before soliciting a bushel of ideas is that a surplus of ideas is just as dangerous as a drought (Belsky, 2010). Jumping from idea to idea spreads your energy thin. This is how progress is stalled. You never fully implement or get the benefit from anything you are implementing.

Perhaps the most important thing for the team to hold as a value and something the leader must keep in focus for everyone is that ideas are great but the point is action. The team must have a relentless bias toward action. And to get action, each team member must "own" his or her action steps (Belsky, 2010). Action steps must be connected to projects, programs, and initiatives. Focus on writing clear, direct action steps. Remember, unowned action steps will never be taken.

Application Activity 4.7

Generating Ideas and Action Steps

Participants: Teams

Conversation Level: This can be a moderate- to high-level conversation for a team. This level of discussion is not typically a good one for a newly formed team. It is best for teams to have some success working together first before exploring this topic.

Purpose: This Activity is designed to connect a team to the importance of making action steps that are reasonable and within their scope to accomplish. The team should be able to have a conversation about times when actions steps weren't made and also times when they were. This is a high-level conversation and should be held only with teams that have worked through other topics in this chapter before arriving here. Teams taking on this conversation before they are prepared may overreach with setting action steps or underreach depending on the relative confidence of the team. Leaders should be prepared by knowing what the team can handle by way of action steps.

Goal: The team should arrive at a place where having a reasonable focus on results is agreed upon and able to be accomplished.

Notes for Future Use: Keep notes on the efficacy of this Activity and the growth seen by team members.

Primary Focus Conversation

What cultural shifts will have to be made to get the team to embrace action steps that are owned and transparent?

Continue the Conversation (Additional Prompts)

1. What preparations will have to be made to get the team able to think about solving problems through a process of generating ideas?

2. What do you anticipate will be the major sources of resistance to generating ideas as a team?

3. How will this resistance be addressed?

Notes

IN THE SCHOOL

▶ *Jefferson Middle School—The principal used this reflection with his Math and English Teams. He recognized that the culture of the school prior to his coming was that low performance from students went unchecked. In working with these teams, he recognized that they would benefit from discussions about beliefs about action steps, culture, ideas, and resistance to ideas.*

DEEPER USE OF THIS CHAPTER: REUSABLE PROMPTS

After working through the content of the chapter, you and your team can now take on some deeper conversations. Use the following prompts as catalysts to explore beliefs and values about leadership, teams, and the purpose of collective work.

DEEPER USE OF THIS CHAPTER: DEEPER DIVES

Leaders are advised to read the entire chapter and explore the Prompts (4.1–4.7) as "pre-work" with your team before arriving at the Deeper Dives. These prompts allow teams to develop some common conversation and thoughts before navigating the deeper water.

Answer the questions below in the context of your team, school, or district depending on the scope and responsibility of your task. Use the tools and reflections from this chapter to bring a greater depth to your team conversation. The questions below should be asked regarding any major initiatives, programs, or proposed solutions in your school or district.

Application Activity 4.8A

Deeper Dive

Participants: Teams

Conversation Level: This conversation is meant for teams that have done much of the other work and conversations in this chapter. It is not advised that a team start here as compared to the other topics in this chapter. This should be used as a culminating conversation.

Purpose: This Activity is designed to help teams solidify their resolve in why systems and processes are most effective for teams to solve problems. The purpose of this discussion is to give teams the time to reflect on the current state and things that may be supporting or not supporting a systems approach to solving problems.

Goal: The use of this topic with a team should provide the end result of teams realizing why sticking with a process and system to work together to solve problems is the most effective and transparent method. Team members should arrive at this topic understanding why they function best as a team and how to sustain their efforts.

Notes for Future Use: Keep notes on the efficacy of this Activity and the growth seen by team members.

Deeper Dive 4.8A—Is there a system and process in place to support the solving of problems in a routine manner? If not, how will this be put in place?

Application Activity 4.8B

Deeper Dive

Participants: Teams

Conversation Level: This conversation is meant for teams that have done much of the other work and conversations in this chapter. It is not advised that a team start here as compared to the other topics in this chapter. This should be used as a culminating conversation.

Purpose: This Activity is designed to help teams solidify their resolve that team structures have everything to do with quality problem solving. The purpose of this discussion is to give teams the time to reflect on the current state and structures that may be impeding the team from deeper problem solving.

Goal: The use of this topic with a team should provide the end result of a team's realizing why structures for the team and structures in the school or district have everything to do with deep solutions and problem solving for the team. This conversation should give teams the collective strength to address structural problems.

Notes for Future Use: Keep notes on the efficacy of this Activity and the growth seen by team members.

Deeper Dive 4.8B—Are there any team structures or behaviors that will have to be improved before meaningful problem solving can take place? If so, what are they and how will you begin to correct them?

Application Activity 4.8C

Deeper Dive

Participants: Teams

Conversation Level: This conversation is meant for teams that have done much of the other work and conversations in this chapter. It is not advised that a team start here as compared to the other topics in this chapter. This should be used as a culminating conversation.

Purpose: This Activity is designed to help teams solidify their resolve as to why the team has to make it a habit to look at every issue from an action-orientation mind-set. Teams must have the skill and training to know that discussing problems without bringing an action orientation means that things will be talked about but nothing will get done or change. Teams must go into every discussion with an eye toward the action that will improve the system.

Goal: The use of this topic with a team should provide the end result of the team's realizing why discussions without action is not a productive use of time for a team.

Notes for Future Use: Keep notes on the efficacy of this Activity and the growth seen by team members.

> Deeper Drive 4.8C—Are the team members trained (and receptive)
> to be action oriented in their approach to problem solving? If not,
> how will the team be trained?

CONCLUSION

Use the tools and reflections from this chapter to bring a greater depth to your team conversation. The questions and Application Activities in this chapter should be asked regarding any and all major initiatives, programs, or proposed solutions in your school or district.

The People Who Will Solve the Problem

5

Using This Chapter

This chapter is for leaders and learning teams who are recognizing that there is a value and importance in the chemistry of the team. This includes the norms of behavior, the expectations about ideas, discussion, and disagreement. Teams that have prolonged and sustained success have mechanisms in place that hold members to standards of behavior and preparation.

If your team or team dynamics has already come to a firm grasp of team chemistry, norms, behavior, and expectations, then this chapter may not be the best use of your team's time.

It is highly recommended that readers using this chapter read the entire chapter first before using one of the Application Activities. This will give a background and perspective on the content and potential needs of the team.

INTRODUCTION

In the previous chapter, we discussed why teams are so important to the process of solving problems and having a proper venue for ideas to surface. The setting matters. The leadership of bringing people together for a common cause matters. Organizations that attend to this structure will outperform those that do not. It's just like a baseball team. A baseball team that works hard practicing the fundamentals of fielding, footwork, throwing, positioning on the field, and situational defense will perform much better game after game than a team that doesn't stick to a structure. That kind of performance leads to more games won over time. It's just the way the game is played. So it is with our organizational teams. Taking time to attend to structure, team dynamics, trust, conflict, commitment, accountability, results, and how ideas are dealt with are the equivalent fundamentals of a baseball team. Fundamentals matter. Just as a baseball coach sets up a practice regimen to expose the team to all the needed skills for a game, so it should be with a school leader. Teams should have background and skill practice on developing a team and having ideas to solve problems before they actually try to do them in a "game" situation.

This chapter will focus on the importance of the people who come to be part of the team. What should be expected of them? What should the leader be expected to do? What should the chemistry of the team be like? How will the team be managed? How will conflict with competing ideas be handled? Each of these questions has potential to stop a team dead in its tracks. Leaders, just like a coach, must be prepared to build and practice the skill sets that provide an antidote to each problem.

Application Activity 5.1

Know How to Build and Use People

Having good people on teams and in organizations is the single most important factor to achieving progress and success. This is especially true in schools and districts. People make the difference. There are some very practical suggestions for managers and leaders to be vigilant of to build the best teams possible.

Find, discover, and harness talent. Leaders must look for talent, discover and identify genius in those around them (Wiseman, Allen, & Foster, 2013). These leaders put talent to use. This mind-set in a leader requires a constant monitoring to discover the many ways that intelligence is manifest, the skills people possess, and how to utilize people at their fullest.

Leaders must come prepared for every meeting and be vigilant in between meetings to be looking for talent and opportunities for people to grow and stretch. This habit of mind changes leaders because they find themselves constantly looking at their people for what they could accomplish next and who could do it. Everything and everyone becomes a hidden opportunity. Leaders with this mind-set are always looking to find it and bring it to light.

> 🔑 **Key Thought**
>
> Leaders must come prepared for every meeting and be vigilant in between meetings to be looking for talent and opportunities for people to grow and stretch.

Create a liberated environment. The last thing you want as a leader developing a team is to create an environment full of stress and anxiety. Leaders should be focused on creating an environment that intensely values thinking and a deep obligation to do their best work (Wiseman et al., 2013). Leaders should build a team where people are given meaningful and challenging tasks, the support needed to be successful, and the freedom to perform. Leaders should allow opportunities to give the team choice and self-direction on carrying out the identified actions. This setup allows for the best thinking and confidence from the team.

> 🔑 **Key Thought**
>
> Leaders should allow opportunities to give the team choice and self-direction on carrying out the identified actions.

A leader with this mind-set about building talent and providing an environment for people to grow, think, challenge, and try is always looking for ways to keep people engaged. Meetings should be active. Meetings should be inclusive. Meetings should revolve around learning, sharing, and going deeper. Mistakes in this kind of environment are shared and discussed not only to learn from the present and support individuals on the team but also to provide a learning opportunity on how the team can avoid this same situation in the future.

Create an environment to challenge thinking and find discoveries. Leaders should always be looking for ways to bring in new thinking to the team. A very important cultural expectation for a team is to bring in new books, articles, or conference reports to share with the team. The exposure to new ideas and thinking can be valuable, often at unpredictable times. Something shared months ago may be recalled and connected to a current problem that brings the perfect fit. If the team missed the exposure to the new thinking, it could be an opportunity lost.

Leaders should fold in time for this kind of sharing and continuous learning in periodic meetings. This kind of structure helps challenge team members to think in new directions and guide new discoveries. Good leaders know that teams, and people want to be stretched, even if they don't come out and ask for it (Wiseman et al., 2013). Leaders have to notice and look for opportunities to give people more challenging work, not just more work. Leaders want teams with broad, expansive thinking. It does no good to have a team comprised of members with limited experience and limited exposure to remedies. Leaders have to expand those qualities in the team.

🔑 **Key Thought**

Leaders have to notice and look for opportunities to give people more challenging work, not just more work.

Build a community. Leaders should keep something in mind: Go slow to go fast. Wanting to make decisions in a small, inner-circle group is of course very efficient. Things get done quickly. Moving from thing to thing is simple. But, as soon as the decision moves out of the learning team to those who will implement the decision, problems arise. People begin to debate the soundness of the decision instead of putting focus on how best to implement it. Leaders or teams who keep others out of the loop on the proposed decision and what it is intended to solve end up spending a great deal of time and energy cleaning it up after the fact instead of investing time to include others from the beginning. Leaders who focus on building a community set up ways to engage people, debate issues, and create transparency long before a decision is put in place (Wiseman et al., 2013).

🔑 **Key Thought**

Leaders or teams who keep others out of the loop on the proposed decision and what it is intended to solve end up spending a great deal of time and energy cleaning it up after the fact instead of investing time to include others from the beginning.

Consider your organization and ways that people can be brought together early in the process of change. Think of ways their thinking can be stretched and prepared. Of course, every decision does not require this type of preparation, but when it comes to major initiatives and programs, it absolutely should be done this way (Wiseman et al., 2013). The more likely a decision is to affect many across the organization, the more important it is to prepare, include, and bring out debate on the matter. Think of it this way: You're going to spend the time one way or the other. Best to spend it up front in discussions and preparation before you are committed to a path, rather than spending time trying to salvage a mess.

Invest in building leaders. People care so much more about the success of something when they own it. When they drive it, care for it, nurture it, and hold responsibility for it's being successful, people make vastly different decisions than when everyone depends on the leader to make all the choices. Leaders and functional teams know that everyone on the team has to hold shared ownership for the programs and initiatives pushed forward.

Leaders have to define ownership and expectations up front and shift the burden of accountability onto others (Wiseman et al., 2013). Discussed in an earlier chapter was the importance of having a results- and an accountability-driven team culture. Giving ownership responsibilities to team members helps to further create this results-driven and accountability-driven culture. People will surpass expectations when shared ownership, results-driven expectations, and transparent accountability are all present. It shouldn't be solely the leader's responsibility to hold people accountable for results. The entire team should be able to function in a way that peers also hold one another accountable for meeting established expectations.

🔑 Key Thought

People will surpass expectations when shared ownership, results-driven expectations, and transparent accountability are all present.

Application Activity 5.1

Know How to Build and Use People

Participants: Teams

Conversation Level: This conversation is best held with an experienced team. Discussions of shared accountability with an unprepared team can be damaging.

(Continued)

(Continued)

Purpose: This Activity is designed to have team members look at the broad picture of who they are and the culture that the team brings. Exploring shared accountability is a topic that can be handled only once trust and conflict understanding have been built. It is advised that the leader or facilitator be vigilant about the timing of when this discussion is held.

Goal: The goal of this Activity is for team members to recognize that having a process for shared accountability is vital. Having shared accountability helps team members perform at a high and effective level because they are intrinsically motivated to support the team.

Notes for Future Use: Take note of team members who struggle more than others when shared accountability is in need of improvement. Some people are reluctant to share when they feel that team members are not being held accountable.

Primary Focus Conversation

What changes will have to be made to bring a culture of shared ownership and accountability to your team(s)?

Continue the Conversation (Additional Prompts)

1. How might you be shutting down the ideas and actions of others despite having the best intentions?

2. What cultural shifts are going to have to take place to set up teams that seek talent and have a liberated environment?

Notes

IN THE SCHOOL

▶ *Washington High School—The principal used this conversation with her Leadership Team. The team had never before held conversations regarding shared ownership of a decision once it is made and the members leave the room. The team had also never talked about how team members are chosen and remain on the team.*

Application Activity 5.2

The Chemistry of the Team

Who you have around you is beyond critical. The team has to be capable. The team has to have initiative. The team has to have drive. The team has to have past success and experiences that can be drawn on to look for parallels. Building a team of enthusiastic and talented people is one of the greatest challenges for leaders (Belsky, 2010). Even beyond the enthusiasm and talent is the ability to work in a team environment. It is ideal to find people who have had past success on teams. Even more critical than past success is to have people who possess initiative to make things happen (Belsky, 2010).

Having a good team is not just important for what the members do but also for what they don't do. Good teams bring good ideas, but they also help dispatch bad ones. Consider that for a moment. Being able to prevent a team from getting off track is a valuable skill. It saves time, money, and energy. One way to help keep a team focused is to have prime goals or a list of team expectations and priorities on the wall of the meeting room. This way, if discussions get too far afield, the team can be easily redirected to what the established targets are.

Discussed earlier in the book was the importance of not having a team made up of identical people. One of the most critical differences to have on a team is at least a person or two who have the ability to see the contrary point of view. As a team develops, it is important to explicitly discuss the importance of skepticism. The proper culture on a team isn't to search for skepticism simply to find it and stop there. It is to address the skeptic's observations and concerns. But, it isn't the point to change the skeptic's mind. Think of it this way: Wouldn't you rather bump into all the barriers inside the safe four walls of your team room than to find the barriers in the middle of your rollout with the entire school or district? In the next chapter, we will explore just how important it is to have a devil's advocate on the team.

> **Key Thought**
>
> As a team develops, it is important to explicitly discuss the importance of skepticism.

Another key chemistry issue that creative teams will run into as they discuss the path forward and the ideas that can take things where they want to go is conflict. It was discussed in a previous chapter, but it cannot be understated. Conflict is critical. Conflict in and of itself is not negative. It becomes negative if it gets personal and there is a lack of norms and structure to channel the conflict in a productive way. If good chemistry has been cultivated, teams can use disagreements to foster valuable insights that would otherwise be inaccessible (Belsky, 2010).

Although discussing conflict, let alone living through it, can be uncomfortable and delicate, there is something worse. The alternative to healthy conflict and disagreement is apathy (Belsky, 2010). This is far more toxic than poorly managed conflict. Apathy leads to team members slowly checking out. Withdrawal from the team and the purpose of the team can deal a lethal blow to the leader, the team, and the organization. Having people lose the will to care is very destructive. As a leader, it is critical to create opportunities for people to debate and argue from different angles. Create mechanisms to get different people with different experience and ability to debate different parts of the idea. Whatever the result of the process, good and healthy teams leave the room in agreement to execute the idea and to put their weight behind it. There can be no halfway. The time for debate is one thing. The time for agreed-upon execution is another. Good teams know when both have occurred.

🔑 Key Thought

Apathy leads to team members slowly checking out. Withdrawal from the team and the purpose of the team can deal a lethal blow to the leader, the team, and the organization.

One very common misconception at this stage of the process is how to bring a debate to a close and create a common execution agreement. The common misconception is consensus. Consensus is a burden and settles on the least common denominator (Belsky, 2010). Consensus usually leads to mediocre outcomes. Consensus is a mechanism where teams are trying to not hurt someone's feelings by including their two cents. Consensus seeks to find common ground, not the best ground. Consensus is not what you're shooting for. This doesn't mean all voices aren't listened to or that all sides aren't considered. In fact, you want to bring in as much input as possible. But, just because all input comes in it doesn't mean it has to find a place at the table as part of the best solution. Some things will be left out because they aren't the best. That's okay. A great team knows this coming in. This process allows for a solution to be exceptional and extraordinary. Consensus will not bring exceptional and extraordinary.

Application Activity 5.2

The Chemistry of the Team

Participant: Leader. Use the prompts below as the primary focus self-reflection. Make note of your responses.

Primary Focus Reflection

Consider the chemistry of your team. Do the members have diversity of experience and problem-solving styles?

Continue the Reflection (Additional Prompts)

1. Does the team have at least one or two devil's advocates? Is their role understood by the rest of the team?

2. What preparation has been made with the team to deal with the common trap of consensus?

Notes

Application Activity 5.3

Managing the Creative Team

Discovering you have a problem is usually not a hard thing to do. In fact, we often have plenty of people, data, and indicators around us to point out that "Houston, we have a problem." It is a rare thing in most schools that a major systemic problem, especially if it is related to teaching and learning, is not widely known. Now, this is not to say that all the details about a problem may be known or that all the ripple effect connections of a problem may be widely known, but the basics of a problem are usually easy to observe. Taking a problem and attaching an idea to it that pushes toward a solution is tricky. This is where the skill comes in.

So far, we have looked at some of the basic components to the situation at hand. That is, identifying the problem. Then, we discussed the ideas that can solve it. Further, we looked at the teams required to solve it. Now, we are looking at the skill sets and abilities of the team being tasked with identifying and solving the problem.

The solution begins with an idea. Some on the team will see, understand, and connect to the problem in a way that they can identify a possible solution. They will have an idea. The first realization to keep in mind is that ideas are not just fragile but they are always in need of nurturing. As discussed earlier, the process with ideas is not to move to consensus. This isn't about wearing people out and coming to a lowest common denominator. This is about trying to find the best answer to your problem. This also means that the first idea may or may not be the best one. What leaders seek is to get as much interest and ownership in the idea as possible. It isn't one person's idea. It has to become everyone's idea. People obsess about ideas only when they feel a sense of ownership (Belsky, 2010).

A word of warning about the leadership of ideas. Most visionary leaders have a common flaw. The common flaw is the tendency to talk first (Belsky, 2010). Leaders have to go into this process with the goal in mind of including the team, connecting everyone to the ownership of the problem and idea for solution. If the leader speaks early, it steers the team away from other possible solutions. It can shut down the creativity of the team to seek more ideas. The overarching goal for a leader is to engage, engage, and engage. The creative process depends on active engagement from the entire team.

🔑 Key Thought

The overarching goal for a leader is to engage, engage, and engage. The creative process depends on active engagement from the entire team.

As discussed earlier in the book, engagement of the team is important but having norms of behavior is critical. The creative process will hit bumps going down the road. It will cause disruption in what people do or think. It will bring out the possibility that the current direction is off-track or less effective than it ought to be. This, if not managed by norms, can cause team members to feel blame or become defensive of their performance. The norms have to be established that this isn't about finger pointing. It is about honest dialogue that if something isn't working, we should look for an improvement. We don't want to keep riding a dead horse. Team members have to have norms to be free to discuss and question their path. But it takes a leader to manage this process.

Application Activity 5.3

Managing the Creative Team

Participants: Teams

Conversation Level: This conversation is best held with an experienced team. Discussions of shared accountability with an unprepared team can be damaging.

Purpose: This Activity is designed to have a team look at the importance of norms and maintaining them. Teams should walk away from this discussion with an understanding that norms help keep teams cohesive, functioning, and accountable. It is critical that all team members share and participate. The only way to create norms and enforce them is to have a collective experience where all members have a vested interest in the outcome.

Goal: The goal of this Activity is for team members to recognize that having a process to create and monitor norms is crucial to the long-term success of the team.

Notes for Future Use: Take note of team members who struggle more than others when norms are not present or are in need of improvement. Some people are reluctant to share when they feel that norms are not being monitored and expected. Note that anytime the team membership changes, norms must be revisited.

Primary Focus Conversation

Does the team have norms not only to support open discussion
but to protect team members from personal attack?

How are teams monitored for genuine engagement and maintenance of norms?

Continue the Conversation (Additional Prompts)

1. How do you as the leader engage a team (or what observations do you make about the leader)?

2. What are the ways that teams have been successfully engaged in the process of problem solving or idea generation?

Notes

IN THE SCHOOL

▶ *Madison Elementary School—The principal used this conversation with her Leadership Team. She wanted to support the team in understanding the importance of having norms to protect members when they share ideas and offer insight.*

Application Activity 5.4

Handling Conflict in the Ideas From the Team

Earlier in the book we looked at the importance of conflict in a team. The "idea" process will bring conflict. Any team that goes after solutions and ideas to a problem and does it conflict-free is not genuinely engaged. People should find themselves activated, and their buttons should be pushed when it comes to solving big issues of teaching and learning. This conversation should cut deep and touch nerves. Use conflict to evaluate the reasoning ability and patience level of the team (Belsky, 2010). Conflict over ideas for solution should be passionate. When the leader sees the team running out of gas or the conflict grows personal or attacking, then the leader has to intervene. The norms of the group should kick in. There is a line where productivity crosses and then becomes personal. It mustn't slip into that.

Leaders should also use conflict as an opportunity to earn the team's respect and confidence (Belsky, 2010). Having a problem, crisis, and/or conflict is a chance for the leader to guide a team through the fire to arrive safely on the other side. This takes trust. It takes monitoring. It takes adherence to the norms. Leaders who use conflict management wisely gain trust and buy goodwill from the team and others in the organization outside of the team. The word spreads. But, the opposite is also true. Leaders who allow conflict to go unchecked or become personal will lose the team. They will also lose in the general organization. Once the goodwill gets damaged or slips away, it will take much more effort to get it back. Treat conflict management wisely, and it will be a powerful tool. Treat it carelessly, and you will endure wounds and scars that can last a very long time.

Key Thought

Leaders who use conflict management wisely gain trust and buy goodwill from the team and others in the organization outside of the team.

Conflict usually surfaces from some common sources. Often, conflict arises due to poor choices of language, ineffective management styles, unclear roles, unclear responsibilities, and false expectations (Cloke & Goldsmith, 2000). Conflict almost certainly brings out and brings with it emotion. Be cautious in acknowledging these feelings. Be sure that the norms of behavior are understood and operating. Use the norms to manage the flow of conversation and emotion. Conflict is necessary. Emotion is a byproduct. Do not stifle the conflict. Do not minimize the emotional connection to the conflict. Allow the process to unfold and be done in a managed and dignified manner. This treatment of conflict will build trust with the team. It shows that the room and team are safe and that people won't be unnecessarily beat up or neglected.

Have some expectations of the management of the conflict before it happens, while it is happening, and after it subsides. First things first, understand the culture and the context of the conflict (Cloke & Goldsmith, 2000). Everyone, especially the leader, must know where this conflict came from and its connection and implication to the organization in both the micro and macro sense. Leaders would be wise to include this in their norms. Understand the source, culture, and context of the conflict. This also builds a sense of trust because the team genuinely tries to understand all the moving parts of the conflict.

During the conflict, it is of course critical to listen and maintain norms to prevent the conflict from becoming personal or attacking. The conflict should remain productive and focused on what is best for the organization and the team. A key behavior to monitor and search for is to look for hidden meanings below the surface of the conflict (Cloke & Goldsmith, 2000). Almost all conflicts have a surface component and then a tangle of below-the-surface issues. Look, listen, and monitor signs for the hidden components of any conflict. They are there. It just requires observation and detection.

After the conflict, take time to do some exploration and debriefing. One of the key items to consider is to learn from difficult behaviors and their impact on the team and the conflict in particular (Cloke & Goldsmith, 2000). This is especially significant if this observation uncovers that the same difficult behaviors seem to arise and come from the same person(s). Leaders would be well advised to keep a notebook with debriefing notes that include this kind of observation. It is one thing to have a conflict. It is another to have a recurring conflict because the same person causes it over and over with his or her behavior or treatment of others. It is a crucial component of this conversation to keep problems separated from people (Cloke & Goldsmith, 2000). A difficult behavior from a person does not discount the fact that they may also have a genuine issue in a conflict. Don't confuse the two.

> 🔑 **Key Thought**
>
> It is one thing to have a conflict. It is another to have a recurring conflict because the same person causes it over and over with his or her behavior or treatment of others.

Ideas will bring passion. Passion will bring emotion. Emotion touches values. This entire path is ripe with conflict possibilities. Leaders and teams have to be prepared in advance that their march toward improvement will bring ideas, and ideas will bring conflict. This is normal and expected. What isn't normal is allowing conflict to go unchecked through a lack of adherence to norms and careful management. Plan for this. This is the only way to push to a level of performance that really makes a difference.

Application Activity 5.4

Handling Conflict in the Ideas From the Team

Participant: Leader. Use the prompts below as the primary focus self-reflection. Make note of your responses.

Primary Focus Reflection

Does the team understand that ideas will bring conflict?

How do you know?

Continue the Reflection (Additional Prompts)

1. What norms and preparations have been made to be ready for conflict before it happens?

2. Do all the team members understand the behavioral expectations when ideas bring out conflict? Does the team have a process observer who can stop the process if the norms are being violated? If you answer no to either of these, stop and make adjustments to the team immediately.

Notes

DEEPER USE OF THIS CHAPTER: DEEPER DIVES

After working through the content of the chapter, you and your team can now take on some deeper conversations. Use the following prompts as catalysts to explore beliefs and values about leadership, teams, and the purpose of collective work.

Leaders are advised to read the entire chapter and explore the Activities as "pre-work" with your team before arriving at the Deeper Dives. The Activities allow teams to develop some common conversation and thoughts before navigating deeper waters.

Answer the questions below in the context of your team, school, and/or district depending on the scope and responsibility of your task. Use the tools and reflections from this chapter to bring a greater depth to your team conversation. The questions below should be asked regarding any and all major initiatives, programs, or proposed solutions in your school or district.

Application Activity 5.5

Deeper Dives

Participant: Leader. Use the prompts below as the primary focus self-reflection. Make note of your responses.

Primary Focus Reflection

How are you, the leader, maximizing each member of the team to put them in the best position possible for maximum productivity (both on the team and for day-to-day responsibilities)?

How are you, the leader, building a team that has a range of strengths and natural skill sets?

Notes

Application Activity 5.6

Deeper Dive

Participants: Teams

Conversation Level: This conversation is meant for teams that have done much of the other work and conversations in this chapter plus previous chapter work on conflict and trust. It is not advised that a team start here as compared to the other topics in this chapter. This should be used as a culminating conversation.

Purpose: This Activity is designed to help teams and the leader reflect on some of the previous work done from the book regarding conflict and the importance of conflict to maximize team function and conclusions. This conversation is meant to allow teams to discuss how conflict surfaces and how it is handled. It is critical for the leader or facilitator to ensure that the conversation does not become personal. It should remain about the business at hand and not focus on a person.

Goal: The use of this topic with a team should provide the end result of teams realizing why having conflict is vital to thoroughly vet decisions and ideas. The conflict should come from a place of people genuinely trying to understand why they are looking for the best path forward. The team should also become more and more comfortable bringing out conflict about ideas and direction.

Notes for Future Use: Keep notes on the efficacy of this Activity and the growth seen by team members.

Primary Focus Conversation

How is conflict used and managed to get the most
out of creative team decisions?

Notes

CONCLUSION

Use the tools and reflections from this chapter to bring a greater depth to your team conversation. The questions and Application Activities in this chapter should be asked regarding any and all major initiatives, programs, or proposed solutions in your school or district.

The People in the Room (the Types)   6

Using This Chapter

This chapter is for leaders and learning teams who are recognizing that there is a value and importance in knowing who is on the team, the skills they bring, and the power of ensuring that all team members share and add to the crafting of ideas and solutions.

If your team or team dynamics has already come to a firm grasp of each person's skill sets and the time and place for them to share, then this chapter may not be the best use of your team's time.

It is highly recommended that readers using this chapter read the entire chapter first before using one of the Application Activities. This will give a background and perspective on the content and potential needs of the team.

INTRODUCTION

As discussed in the previous chapters, it should be clear and obvious that it matters a great deal who is in the room. It matters that there be diversity of thought. It matters that there be diversity of experience. It matters that there be diversity of expertise. It matters that the team have time and training to function as a team. It matters that the team have trust and know how to productively use conflict.

This chapter will add yet one more layer of consideration as to who you have on the team. It matters that one of the important things the leader looks for in a team is how team members approach problems and ideas. Everyone has different strategies and talents when it comes to problems and ideas. Knowing what people tend to do will help a team lean on different people at different times to keep a process moving. Said another way, people bring natural strengths, whether they come from personality or experience. Learning leaders and learning teams are best served knowing and working from places of strength.

For purposes of simplicity, this chapter will subdivide the team members based on four characteristics. It is important to say that this subdivision is not absolute. Leaders and teams must know that this is only a "scratch the surface" tool. People and their abilities are much more complex than anything that one simple assessment and description can provide. But, as a starting place, this assessment and resulting descriptors can lead to conversation and awareness of how different team members can become very important at different times in any problem-solving, idea-generating, or initiative-implementing situation. In other words, at different times different team members become the key to progress and success. The trick is knowing who the team should be listening to the most and when.

THE ASSESSMENT

To get this chapter started, each team member will take a short, four-part assessment. Follow the directions, take the assessment, and score each section before moving on to the next. Immediately following the assessment will be the narrative explanations of the different "types" in the room and how they can be used for maximum gain.

Type 1

Answer each pair of descriptors by selecting one that *most* matches your personality or characteristics. Note: This is not an absolute. You may find that several questions do not match you exactly. If this is the case, select the choice that you tend to lean toward or use most often.

Which do you prefer?

   A) Are you more energized when you are getting tasks done?

OR

   B) Are you more energized by thinking and talking about the ideas of what needs to be done?

Selection _____

Which do you prefer?

C) Are you more connected to a task when you know that the system is built right and all the mechanics are thought through?

OR

D) Are you more connected to a task when action is being taken and the work is visibly under way?

Selection _____

Which do you prefer?

E) Are you "more action, less talk"?

OR

F) Are you more concerned that the action fits with other tasks to be sure there is no disruption to other areas of the organization?

Selection _____

Which do you prefer?

G) Are you more interested in getting tasks assigned?

OR

H) Are you more interested in talking about how ideas connect together?

Selection _____

Which do you prefer?

I) Do you not mind the ambiguity of tasks in various stages of development?

OR

J) Do you prefer the concrete conclusion from having a task completed with minimal ambiguity?

Selection _____

Collect your five responses from this section below for Type 1.

Selection A or B	Selection C or D	Selection E or F	Selection G or H	Selection I or J

Type 2

Answer each pair of descriptors by selecting one that *most* matches your personality or characteristics. Note: This is not an absolute. You may find that several questions do not match you exactly. If this is the case, select the choice that you tend to lean toward or use most often.

Which is most like you?

K) I like to know all of the details about the task being worked on

OR

L) I like to know what the end destination looks like

Selection _____

Which is most like you?

M) Knowing how and why multiple things fit together is very important to me.

OR

N) Knowing the clear purpose and direction of the one thing I'm working on now is very important to me.

Selection _____

Which is most like you?

O) I would rather know about the tree in front of me now.

OR

P) I would rather have an understanding about the entire forest.

Selection _____

Which is most like you?

Q) I do my best work when I can visualize how a task interacts with all other tasks in the organization.

OR

R) I do my best work when I think through every step of a task, prioritize them one by one, and execute them.

Selection _____

Which is most like you?

S) I am most comfortable describing how ideas connect (connecting the dots).

OR

T) I am most comfortable working on the task at hand (one piece at a time).

Selection _____

Collect your five responses from this section below for Type 2.

Selection K or L	Selection M or N	Selection O or P	Selection Q or R	Selection S or T

Type 3

Answer each pair of descriptors by selecting one that *most* matches your personality or characteristics. Note: This is not an absolute. You may find that several questions do not match you exactly. If this is the case select the choice that you tend to lean toward or use most often.

Which is most like you?

U) I am okay being in the messiness of a project during the building stages.

OR

V) I prefer the finished product.

Selection _____

Which is most like you?

W) I don't mind the ambiguity of not knowing exactly how everything turns out.

OR

X) I like projects with clear conclusions.

Selection _____

Which is most like you?

Y) I like the "sure thing."

OR

Z) I can live in uncertainty.

Selection _____

Which is most like you?

AA) I like knowing exactly where we are going and how we are going
to get there.

OR

BB) I don't mind working out the details as we go.

Selection _____

Which is most like you?

CC) I believe that time spent "in the process" should lead to a clear set
of steps.

OR

DD) I am okay if time spent leads to more questions and discussion
with no clear-cut direction.

Selection _____

Collect your five responses from this section below for Type 3.

Selection U or V	Selection W or X	Selection Y or Z	Selection AA or BB	Selection CC or DD

Type 4

Answer each pair of descriptors by selecting one that *most* matches your
personality or characteristics. Note: This is not an absolute. You may find
that several questions do not match you exactly. If this is the case, select
the choice that you tend to lean toward or use most often.

Which is most like you?

EE) I know that everything has a "failure point."

OR

FF) I prefer to see the possibility of things and programs working.
Selection _____

Which is most like you?

GG) I tend to think that things work more often than they fail.

OR

HH) I am comfortable discussing what a broken program looks like.
Selection _____

Which is most like you?

II) I don't mind playing the pessimist role.

OR

JJ) I prefer to play the optimist role.
Selection _____

Which is most like you?

KK) I can easily see "the other side."

OR

LL) I prefer to look for the reasons why something will work and the
benefit to be derived when it does.
Selection _____

Which is most like you?

MM) I don't care for conflict in discussing ideas.

OR

NN) I don't mind if there is conflict, and I don't mind if I bring the
contrarian point of view.
Selection _____

Collect your five responses from this section below for Type 4.

Selection EE or FF	Selection GG or HH	Selection II or JJ	Selection KK or LL	Selection MM or NN

THE BASICS

Again, this chapter is built around the observation that different team members have different skills. They have different ranges of experience. They have different abilities to draw on their skills to solve problems in the present. What is most important for a leader to keep in mind is that all of the different skills are critical at different stages of the idea development and problem-solving process. This chapter comes from that place. It is a brief and simple way of providing a quick inventory on which skill sets you have in the room. This also provides a process to be certain that everyone in the room has a chance to speak from their skill set strengths.

The four types fit into this equation: Making ideas happen = the idea + organization and execution + forces of community + leadership capacity (Belsky, 2010). Using this equation, we can extend the thinking into categorizing the four parts or types.

Application Activity 6.1

Part 1/Type 1: The Idea

Earlier in the book, we discussed how ideas come to light. A process of identifying that there is a problem should lead to ideas to solve the problem. Think for a moment not about having ideas but how different people bring different skill sets to the "having ideas" phase. Some people are more prone to and enjoy thinking of ideas. They are energized by having and thinking of ideas. It may be effortless for them. It doesn't mean that all the ideas are good. It just means they can creatively come up with many ideas and possibilities. Let's call these people the Inventors. This type is most valuable in the beginning of the process. They can generate many choices and possibilities.

There is a counter-balance to the Inventor. This type is energized by getting ideas into motion. They see steps and increments. They attach details to ideas. They are energized by getting things in action. They may or may not be overwhelmed by the mass generation of ideas that the Inventor brings, but what they do well is bring a sense of action and reality to the ideas. These people are the Movers. They want action. They want a decision made and a path chosen. That is when they are at their best. They flourish when the train begins to leave the station. They push the team toward and into action.

Refer back to Type 1 and the assessment. Place your selections in the appropriate columns.

Selection	Your Choice (I)			Selection	Your Choice (M)
B		Or	A		
C		Or	D		
F		Or	E		
H		Or	G		
I		Or	J		
Total of Column				Total of Column	

In the above grid, if your score is greater in column I than it is in column M you are an Inventor. Likewise, if column M is greater than column I you are a Mover.

Which category do you manifest? (Inventor or Mover) _____

It should be mentioned again that this assessment and identification is not an absolute. You may have strong skill sets in both. You may have less developed skill sets in both. But, for purposes of the team, it is useful to have different people identified to fill different roles. Strengths and tendencies are important to know about team members. Also, it is important to note that relative tendency is also important. If you score 5 out of 5 in the Inventor or Mover category, it may signal a very strong tendency as a strength. The reverse is also true. If a team member scores a 3 in one and a 2 in the other, it may signal that the two skill sets are either equally developed or that these two items are not an area that this person has a strong affinity to. In any event, it is important to have a conversation regarding the results of this brief assessment.

Application Activity 6.1

Part 1/Type 1: The Idea

Participants: Teams

Conversation Level: This Activity is not recommended for a beginning team (trust and foundational skill are needed first). But, this is an excellent place to start with a team that is moving beyond the beginning stages of being a team. It is excellent for teams that are ready for a positive confidence-building conversation after basic team skills are present.

Groundwork: The team must have taken the short diagnostics in this chapter before beginning the conversations. It is advised to complete the entire set of four diagnostics before hosting these Activities. Allow ample time for each of the four diagnostic areas to hold their corresponding conversation. It is important for the team to have the time and space to discuss the things that come to mind.

Purpose: This Activity is designed to maximize a team's efforts when examining a program, service, or initiative. Ideally, this conversation is held before the team, school, or district has committed funds, people, and effort to the cause. This Activity and the others in this chapter are designed to get all members of the team activated and discussing their thoughts from specific points of view.

Goal: The conclusion of this effort should be that a program, service, or initiative has been discussed and looked at from some very important contrasting points of view. There is no wrong way for a team to discuss these ideas and reflection other than to skip it. The leader or facilitator should be observant that every member on both sides of the conversation gets a chance to engage and have the floor.

Notes for Future Use: Keep notes on who identified with each of the four diagnostic areas. These identifiers can be helpful in future team situations.

Primary Focus Conversation

Have the group discuss who is the room is an Inventor.

How many 5s, 4s, and 3s are there? How accurate is that reading of them?

Do the same with Movers.

How many 5s, 4s, and 3s are there? How accurate is that reading of them?

Continue the Conversation (Additional Prompts)

1. Select a program or initiative that is under way now in your school or district that is big, long-term, and/or has complicated moving parts. To understand the situation surrounding this program or initiative, consider the team dynamics of Movers and Inventors and the role they could play to better support this program or initiative.

2. Discuss the program/initiative from both sides of the continuum: Movers and Inventors. Give both sides opportunities to examine current status, next steps, and concerns.

Notes

IN THE SCHOOL

► *This assessment and the results are meant to give a team and leader a small glimpse into the diversity of the team. Knowing who on the team possesses skill or strength in an area can help a team explore ideas and solutions from multiple angles to vet the solution to make it the best it can be.*

Application Activity 6.2

Part 2/Type 2: Organization and Execution

Following the above section about having the ideas (Inventors and Movers) comes the challenge in an organization of being certain that the idea is properly fleshed out. Some people in the room will have a strength in seeing and describing details. These people usually find it effortless to think of a task or an idea and break it down into all of its component parts. These people enjoy details. They are the Trees. They understand that there is a forest but the individual trees matter most. They have a natural pull toward being sure all the details are described, charted, and listed. The Trees are crucial to a team to be sure that no stone remains unturned in the river bed. They will see missing parts. They will alert the team that "something is missing."

The other side of this coin is the Forests. These people do not get energized by details. They see the whole forest. They see things from 30,000 feet.

The Forests will be the team members who alert the team that entire projects do or don't fit together. They will connect dots from a distance. They will be most valuable when they are tasked with describing how big projects will or won't mesh with other parts of the organization. They often do not get lost in specifics of dollars, people, or metrics. The Forests understand broad strokes and help the team be sure that things work in the "big picture."

Refer back to Type 2 and the assessment. Place your selections in the appropriate columns.

Selection	Your Choice (T)		Selection	Your Choice (F)
K		Or	L	
N		Or	M	
O		Or	P	
R		Or	Q	
T		Or	S	
Total of Column			Total of Column	

In the above grid, if your score is greater in column T than it is in column F you are a Tree. Likewise, if column F is greater than column T you are a Forest.

Which category do you manifest? (Tree or Forest) _____

It should be mentioned again that this assessment and identification is not an absolute. You may have strong skill sets in both. You may have less developed skill sets in both. But, for purposes of the team, it is useful to have different people identified to fill different roles. Strengths and tendencies are important to know about team members. Also, it is important to note that relative tendency is also important. If you score 5 out of 5 in the Tree or Forest category, it may signal a very strong tendency as a strength. The reverse is also true. If a team member scores a 3 in one and a 2 in the other, it may signal that the two skill sets are either equally developed or that these two items are not an area that this person has a strong affinity to. In any event, it is important to have a conversation regarding the results of this brief assessment.

Application Activity 6.2

Part 2/Type 2: Organization and Execution

Participants: Teams

Conversation Level: This Activity is not recommended for a beginning team (trust and foundational skill are needed first). But, this is an excellent place to start with a team that is moving beyond the beginning stages of being a team. It is excellent for teams that are ready for a positive confidence-building conversation after basic team skills are present.

Groundwork: The team must have taken the short diagnostics in this chapter before beginning the conversations. It is advised to complete the entire set of four diagnostics before hosting these process prompts. Allow ample time for each of the four diagnostic areas to hold their corresponding conversation. It is important for the team to have the time and space to discuss the things that come to mind.

Purpose: This Activity is designed to maximize a team's efforts when examining a program, service, or initiative. Ideally, this conversation is held before the team, school, or district has committed funds, people, and effort to the cause. This Activity and the others in this chapter are designed to get all members of the team activated and discussing their thoughts from specific points of view.

Goal: The conclusion of this effort should be that a program, service, or initiative has been discussed and looked at from some very important contrasting points of view. There is no wrong way for a team to discuss these ideas and reflection other than to skip it. The leader or facilitator should be observant that every member on both sides of the conversation gets a chance to engage and have the floor.

Notes for Future Use: Keep notes on who identified with each of the four diagnostic areas. These identifiers can be helpful in future team situations.

Primary Focus Conversation

Have the group discuss who is the room is a Tree.

How many 5s, 4s, and 3s are there? How accurate is that reading of them?

Do the same with Forests.

How many 5s, 4s, and 3s are there? How accurate is that reading of them?

Continue the Conversation (Additional Prompts)

1. Select a program or initiative that is under way now in your school or district that is big, long-term, and/or has complicated moving parts. To understand the situation surrounding this program or initiative, consider the team dynamics of

(Continued)

(Continued)

Trees and Forests and the role they could play to better support this program or initiative.

2. Discuss the program/initiative from both sides of the continuum: Trees and Forests. Give both sides opportunities to examine current status, next steps, and concerns.

Notes

IN THE SCHOOL

▶ *This assessment and the results are meant to give a team and leader a small glimpse into the diversity of the team. Knowing who on the team possesses skill or strength in an area can help a team explore ideas and solutions from multiple angles to vet the solution to make it the best it can be.*

Application Activity 6.3

Part 3/Type 3: Forces of Community

Following the above section about organizing and executing the ideas (Trees and Forests) comes the challenge in an organization of being certain that the idea is properly nourished and fertilized along the way. Recall that Type 1 (Inventors and Movers) focused on having the idea and getting an idea pushed into motion. Type 2 (Trees and Forests) brings different skill sets to take an idea and vet it both from a distance and from tight details. Type 3 now assumes that there is an idea, that it is in motion, and that it has been thought through as to how it fits in the big picture and the detailed little picture.

Type 3 focuses on the skill sets needed to keep an idea alive. One skill set comes from the people on the team who don't mind the messiness of the growth process. If we think of this in terms of a garden, some people are very good and patient to observe and support the garden as it grows. These people are the Growers. They don't mind uncertainty (how many plants will make it to the harvest). They don't mind pulling weeds along the way. They don't mind measuring and monitoring for water levels, fertilizer usage, and sunlight availability. So it is with a new program or initiative. Some people are skilled at being sure that the people and resources are monitored to be sure everyone and everything is doing okay along the way. They are the ones to be sure that if people are anxious or unsure about what to do, they help to get them back to feeling clear and confident. Every team and program has to have a Grower. Gardens need attention and care. So do programs. Growers gravitate to this and have the skill sets to accomplish it.

The other side of the coin is those who do not care for or do well in the ambiguity and uncertainty of the growing phase. They are more comfortable coming into the garden when it is time to harvest. Harvesters like the finished product. They are skilled at describing what they expect. They know what it should look like and can keep a team pointed in the direction of the target. They usually don't do well with ambiguity. Harvesters don't care for the messiness of the nourishment of the garden along the way. They like things to be done, measured, and quantified.

Refer back to Type 3 and the assessment. Place your selections in the appropriate columns.

Selection	Your Choice (G)		Selection	Your Choice (H)
V		Or	U	
W		Or	X	
Z		Or	Y	
AA		Or	BB	
CC		Or	DD	
Total of Column			Total of Column	

In the above grid, if your score is greater in Column G than it is in Column H you are a Grower. Likewise, if Column H is greater than Column G you are a Harvester.

Which category do you manifest? (Grower or Harvester) _____

It should be mentioned again that this assessment and identification is not an absolute. You may have strong skill sets in both. You may have less developed skill sets in both. But, for purposes of the team, it is useful to have different people identified to fill different roles. Strengths and tendencies are important to know about team members. Also, it is important to note that relative tendency is also important. If you score 5 out of 5 in the Grower or Harvest category, it may signal a very strong tendency as a strength. The reverse is also true. If a team member scores a 3 in one and a 2 in the other, it may signal that the two skill sets are either equally developed or that these two items are not an area that this person has a strong affinity to. In any event, it is important to have a conversation about the results of this brief assessment.

Application Activity 6.3

Part 3/Type 3: Forces of Community

Participants: Teams

Conversation Level: This Activity is not recommended for a beginning team (trust and foundational skill are needed first). But this is an excellent place to start with a team that is moving beyond the beginning stages of being a team. It is excellent for teams that are ready for a positive confidence-building conversation after basic team skills are present.

Groundwork: The team must have taken the short diagnostics in this chapter before beginning the conversations. It is advised to complete the entire set of four diagnostics before hosting these process prompts. Allow ample time for each of the four diagnostic areas to hold their corresponding conversation. It is important for the team to have the time and space to discuss the things that come to mind.

Purpose: This Activity is designed to maximize a team's efforts when examining a program, service, or initiative. Ideally, this conversation is held before the team, school, or district has committed funds, people, and effort to the cause. This Activity and the others in this chapter are designed to get all members of the team activated and discussing their thoughts from specific points of view.

Goal: The conclusion of this effort should be that a program, service, or initiative has been discussed and looked at from some very important contrasting points of view. There is no wrong way for a team to discuss these ideas and reflection other than to skip it. The leader or facilitator should be observant that every member on both sides of the conversation gets a chance to engage and have the floor.

Notes for Future Use: Keep notes on who identified with each of the four diagnostic areas. These identifiers can be helpful in future team situations.

Primary Focus Conversation

Have the group discuss who is the room is a Grower. How many 5s, 4s, and 3s are there? How accurate is that reading of them?

Do the same with Harvesters.

How many 5s, 4s, and 3s are there? How accurate is that reading of them?

Continue the Conversation (Additional Prompts)

1. Select a program or initiative that is under way now in your school or district that is big, long-term, and/or has complicated moving parts. To understand the situation surrounding this program or initiative, consider the team dynamics of Growers and Harvesters and the role they could play to better support this program or initiative.

2. Discuss the program/initiative from both sides of the continuum: Growers and Harvesters. Give both sides opportunities to examine current status, next steps, and concerns.

Notes

_____

IN THE SCHOOL

▶ *This assessment and the results are meant to give a team and leader a small glimpse into the diversity of the team. Knowing who on the team possesses skill or strength in an area can help a team explore ideas and solutions from multiple angles to vet the solution to make it the best it can be.*

Application Activity 6.4

Part 4/Type 4: Leadership Capacity

Following the above section about growing or harvesting the ideas would seem to be the end of the road. The harvest has been brought in. What more is there to discuss? Well, along the way and threaded throughout is the needed skill of leadership. Ideas and the implementing of them don't happen without effort and care. Ideas require leadership. Ideas require guidance and scrutiny. Failure to do both can prove lethal to a fledgling idea.

One crucial voice to have in the room from the very beginning is the contrarian one. Sometimes referred to as the devil's advocate, this voice plays a key role of bringing the unexpected point of view. This Devil is absolutely crucial. A fatal flaw on a team is when an idea is brought forward and it starts to take shape, and everyone on the team is excited and in favor of it. But, what if no one ever stopped to consider what it would look like if it failed? No one stopped to think about how this will look from people's point of view who are less than excited. The devil's advocate brings a voice to make the group consider the harsh alternative. What if the program isn't well received? What if hard times come? This voice makes an idea and implemented program stronger by poking holes in it while it is still in the room. This isn't to say that once all the concerns have been raised, the Devil doesn't back the program 100%. It's just that their role is to voice the least desirable possibilities. Every team *must* have at least one person skilled at this role.

The other side of the coin from the Devil is the Champion. Every idea and program must have a Champion. This person isn't just in favor of the program—this person becomes the public face of the program. He or she is the owner and leads it. The Champion is the optimist force behind it. This person manages it and rallies forces to support it. The Champion monitors its performance. The Champion alerts the group when support is needed. The Champion also carries the task of organizing celebrations when success is seen. This person has to be the optimist for the program. The Champion will try to mitigate conflict in the program once it has been vetted by the devil's advocate. Every program must have a Champion.

Refer back to Type 4 and the assessment. Place your selections in the appropriate columns.

Selection	Your Choice (D)		Selection	Your Choice (C)
EE		Or	FF	
HH		Or	GG	
II		Or	JJ	
KK		Or	LL	
NN		Or	MM	
Total of Column			Total of Column	

In the above grid, if your score is greater in Column D than it is in Column C you are a Devil. Likewise, if Column C is greater than Column D you are a Champion.

Which category do you manifest? (Devil or Champion) _____

It should be mentioned again that this assessment and identification is not an absolute. You may have strong skill sets in both. You may have less developed skill sets in both. But, for purposes of the team, it is useful to have different people identified to fill different roles. Strengths and tendencies are important to know about team members. It is important to note that relative tendency is also important. If you score 5 out of 5 in the Devil or Champion category, it may signal a very strong tendency as a strength. The reverse is also true. If a team member scores a 3 in one and a 2 in the other, it may signal either that the two skill sets are equally developed or that these two items are not an area that this person has a strong affinity to. In any event, it is important to have a conversation about the results of this brief assessment.

Application Activity 6.4

Part 4/Type 4: Leadership Capacity

Participants: Teams

Conversation Level: This Activity is not recommended for a beginning team (trust and foundational skill are needed first). But this is an excellent place to start with

(Continued)

(Continued)

a team that is moving beyond the beginning stages of being a team. It is excellent for teams that are ready for a positive confidence-building conversation after basic team skills are present.

Groundwork: The team must have taken the short diagnostics in this chapter before beginning the conversations. It is advised to complete the entire set of four diagnostics before hosting these process prompts. Allow ample time for each of the four diagnostic areas to hold their corresponding conversation. It is important for the team to have the time and space to discuss the things that come to mind.

Purpose: This Activity is designed to maximize a team's efforts when examining a program, service, or initiative. Ideally, this conversation is held before the team, school, or district has committed funds, people, and effort to the cause. This activity and the others in this chapter are designed to get all members of the team activated and discussing their thoughts from specific points of view.

Goal: The conclusion of this effort should be that a program, service, or initiative has been discussed and looked at from some very important contrasting points of view. There is no wrong way for a team to discuss these ideas and reflection other than to skip it. The leader or facilitator should be observant that every member on both sides of the conversation gets a chance to engage and have the floor.

Notes for Future Use: Keep notes on who identified with each of the four diagnostic areas. These identifiers can be helpful in future team situations.

Primary Focus Conversation

Have the group discuss who is the room is a Devil.

How many 5s, 4s, and 3s are there? How accurate is that reading of them?

Do the same with Champion.

How many 5s, 4s, and 3s are there? How accurate is that
reading of them?

Continue the Conversation (Additional Prompts)

1. Select a program or initiative that is under way now in your school or district that is big, long-term, and/or has complicated moving parts. To understand the situation surrounding this program or initiative, consider the team dynamics of Devils and Champions and the roles they could play to better support this program or initiative.

2. Discuss the program/initiative from both sides of the continuum: Devils and Champions. Give both sides opportunities to examine current status, next steps, and concerns.

Notes

IN THE SCHOOL

▶ *This assessment and the results are meant to give a team and leader a small glimpse into the diversity of the team. Knowing who on the team possesses skill or strength in an area can help a team explore ideas and solutions from multiple angles to vet the solution to make it the best it can be.*

USING THE FOUR TYPES

Each person on the team should now have the four types identified. Take a moment and place your information in the grid below.

The Idea	The Organization and Execution of the Idea	The Forces of Community Around the Idea	Leadership Capacity to Support the Idea
Movers = M Inventors = I Place your letter in the box below.	Trees = T Forests = F Place your letter in the box below.	Growers = G Harvesters = H Place your letter in the box below.	Devils = D Champions = C Place your letter in the box below.

Remember, these four letters or types are not absolute. The purpose of this is to involve different team members at different points along the way of generating an idea and moving a resulting program choice into implementation.

The most important thing for a leader or team member to understand is that along the path of problem → idea → program, each of the four types plays a part. None of them can be skipped or overlooked. This scrutiny is what allows for the best final product to come forward. It is this process that allows for the possibility of solid implementation. If these basic skill sets are not present on a team, then it is almost certain that time will be squandered, money will be wasted, and energy will be misspent.

CONCLUSION

Use the tools and reflections from this chapter to bring a greater depth to your team conversation. The questions and Application Activities in this chapter should be asked regarding any and all major initiatives, programs, or proposed solutions in your school or district. These activities will build better teams, foster greater understanding of individual skill sets, and create an environment for all team members to participate and collectively build the direction that will serve students better.

PART III

Functionality of the Team

People, Leadership, 7 Support (the Fuel Sources)

Using This Chapter

This chapter is for leaders and learning teams who are recognizing that there is a value and importance in having a keen understanding of the people, the leadership, and the supports available to aid in implementing and installing programs and services that impact student learning.

If your team or team dynamics has already come to a firm grasp of how to support and sustain implementation, then this chapter may not be the best use of your team's time.

It is highly recommended that readers using this chapter read the entire chapter first before using one of the Application Activities. This will give a background and perspective on the content and potential needs of the team.

INTRODUCTION

Implementing and sustaining a program or initiative is an ongoing and dynamic process. It is not static. It changes and shifts every day. Every new variable shifts the balance slightly. Leaders and teams must be constantly vigilant to observe and take note of any development. Failure to take into account the changing and shifting environment can lead to irreparable harm.

Because schools are constantly changing and evolving, it is critical that leaders and teams take time to notice how things interplay. Further, it is imperative that leaders and teams understand their responsibility to feed and nourish the programs and initiatives. In fact, it is so critical to the long-term health and survival of a program that teams should regularly discuss the fuel sources required to keep a program alive.

In much the same way the human body requires a variety of vitamins and minerals to carry out the many chemical reactions, programs and initiatives have some "dietary" requirements as well. Programs and initiatives require regular fuel and maintenance. Simply purchasing and installing a program or initiative does not guarantee its use or success. In the same vein, sending teachers and staff to a one-shot professional development on how to use the program or initiative is a start, but it will not suffice. The human body requires constant fuel and maintenance to run at optimal levels. Cars are the same way. Gasoline, regular oil changes, and routine maintenance keep cars running and performing well for years. Why should we think of programs or initiatives any differently?

This chapter focuses on the basic things to keep programs and initiatives performing at an optimal level. In fact, Fixsen and Blase (2015) describe the ingredients seen when implementation "works." They go on to label these things in three categories of "implementation drivers": Competency, Organization, and Leadership (Fixsen & Blase, 2015). To summarize, good implementation takes into account these three implementation driver categories—Competency (People), Organization (Supports), and Leadership—and accounts for the moving parts in each. To do that we will consider the discussion from these three basic directions: Fuel Source A, The People; Fuel Source B, The Resource of Leadership; and Fuel Source C, The Supports. Each of these fuel sources is crucial in its own right. But, the true power is having a system where all three fuel sources can be revisited on a regular basis to check on the "health" of a given program or initiative.

FUEL SOURCE A: THE PEOPLE

Background

People are an obvious and necessary resource. Nothing gets done without having the right people in the right places at the right times. The art and science of implementing and sustaining programs and initiatives depends very heavily on the people in your organization. The people attached to working with a program or initiative make a tremendous difference as to how successful the results will be. We will examine the importance of people through three lenses: (1) who, (2) what, and (3) how.

Application Activity 7.1

Who

It is a critical function and step in any program: Who will be tasked with making it function and come together? The leader and team should be mindful of the many ramifications of this decision. Very often schools end up giving the most to do to the same few people. Is this the best choice? Perhaps. Perhaps not. Discussion should be held to debate the best path forward. To best answer the question of "who," first think of what the program should look like at full build-out. Then work backward to the present day and think through how the rollout will unfold. Finally, consider which people connect to the build-out and the effect of their roles.

Application Activity 7.1

Who

Participants: Teams

Conversation Level: This Activity is not recommended for a beginning team (trust and foundational skill are needed first). But this is an excellent place to start with a team that is moving beyond the beginning stages of being a team. It is excellent for teams that are ready for a positive confidence-building conversation after basic team skills are present.

Purpose: This Activity is designed to have a team look at the broad picture of the programs and services they either provide now or are considering to include. This conversation helps the team members think through the logistics and rationale behind how they bring in and support a program. Be advised: These topics will likely bring out a broader look at what it takes to support a program or service. These conversations help a team realize that a new program or service will take a great deal of time and effort to get it to full implementation.

Goal: The goal of this Activity is for team members to recognize that having a process to train staff on installing a new program is vital. Discussing the rollout plan is crucial for the connectedness of the team.

Notes for Future Use: Keep notes on the efficacy of this Activity and the growth seen by team members. Take note of team members who struggle more than others when shared accountability is in need of improvement. Some people are reluctant to share when they feel that team members are not being held accountable.

(Continued)

(Continued)

Primary Focus Conversation

Select a program/initiative or a potential program/initiative that either is under way or could be added in your school or district. Select a program/initiative or a problem that is big, long-term, and/or has complicated moving parts.

Will the program be rolled out in phases?

Will phases impact which staff members are brought on and at which time?

Continue the Conversation (Additional Prompts)

1. Does the program require special requisite training, credentials, or certifications?

2. Do some staff members have these qualifications?

3. Are any staff members unqualified?

4. Is the program designed to expand to the whole staff?

Notes

IN ACTION: SUGGESTED USE

▶ *These prompts are built to provide a leader and a guiding team the conversation regarding selection of programs or evaluation of programs. These prompts are designed to bring out conversation to be sure that a selected program, idea, or solution is truly the best use of time, money, and energy, and that it is implemented well.*

Application Activity 7.2

What

Most programs and initiatives (especially if purchased from a vendor or provider) come with some professional development as part of the package.

The details of this training should be considered first. What will the scope be? How deep will it be? How many staff members will be involved? A key detail to understand is how far will the training go to get the program off the ground? Very often, the opening trainings are superficial and designed to simply get people started. Although this is a critical first step, this initial training will not suffice. Deeper layers of training will be needed, and usually in rapid succession. The leader and team must plan this out from the beginning. Take into account the resources needed to host a series of trainings to support the program.

Application Activity 7.2

What

Participants: Teams

Conversation Level: This Activity is not recommended for a beginning team (trust and foundational skill are needed first). But this is an excellent place to start with a team that is moving beyond the beginning stages of being a team. It is excellent for teams that are ready for a positive confidence-building conversation after basic team skills are present.

Purpose: This Activity is designed to have a team look at the broad picture of the programs and services they either provide now or are considering to include. This conversation helps the team members think through the logistics and rationale behind how they bring in and support a program. Be advised: These topics will likely bring out a broader look at what it takes to support a program or service. These conversations help a team realize that a new program or service will take a great deal of time and effort to get it to full implementation.

Goal: The goal of this discussion is for team members to recognize that having a process to train staff on installing a new program is vital. Discussing the rollout plan is crucial for the connectedness of the team.

Notes for Future Use: Keep notes on the efficacy of this Activity and the growth seen by team members. Take note of team members who struggle more than others when discussions of training and implementation of the training take place. Very often professional development is done to staff just in case instead of just in time. Keep in mind that some team members may have had some negative past experiences.

Primary Focus Conversation

Select a program/initiative or a potential program/initiative that either is under way or could be added in your school or district. Select a program/initiative or a problem that is big, long-term, and/or has complicated moving parts.

(Continued)

(Continued)

What will the training prepare staff to do?

Will staff be able to begin implementation after the training? If so, how deeply?

Continue the Conversation (Additional Prompts)

1. Are follow-up trainings required? How many?

2. Are resources set aside to accomplish this?

3. How many trainings will be needed to get staff to the point of being proficient at operating the program?

4. Is the training able to be learned by staff and then delivered to others (trainer of trainers)?

Notes

Application Activity 7.3

How (Coaching)

Once training is provided, then a crucial step follows: coaching. Being around schools and districts for any amount of time brings a very up close view of this reality. The scrap heap of attempted programs and initiatives is full of examples where things started off with a bang, only to fizzle and fade due to lack of ongoing support. Teaching is a difficult craft. Expecting teachers to fold in a new technique or set of materials to their repertoire without support is foolhardy at best. It is destructive at its worst. Dollars must be set aside in advance to support ongoing contact, training, and on-the-job coaching. This amount of attention and support sends a clear message that the program is important and valued. Leaders must set a clear expectation that programs be used, coaching be provided, and things be put into practice.

Key Thought

Expecting teachers to fold in a new technique or set of materials to their repertoire without support is foolhardy at best. It is destructive at its worst.

Application Activity 7.3

How (Coaching)

Participants: Teams

Conversation Level: This Activity is not recommended for a beginning team (trust and foundational skill are needed first). But this is an excellent place to start with a team that is moving beyond the beginning stages of being a team. It is excellent for teams that are ready for a positive confidence-building conversation after basic team skills are present.

Purpose: This Activity is designed to have a team reflect on the importance of ongoing coaching that comes after a training. This conversation is used to help a team plan for a long-range implementation and realize that to sustain any program or service, it requires coaching to provide feedback and support on proper use of the new system. Be advised: These topics will likely bring out a broader look at what it takes to support a program or service. These conversations help a team realize that a new program or service will take a great deal of time and effort to get it to full implementation.

Goal: The goal of this discussion is for team members to recognize that having a process to coach and support staff on installing a new program is vital. Discussing the rollout plan is crucial for connectedness of the team.

Notes for Future Use: Keep notes on the efficacy of this Activity and the growth seen by team members. Take note of team members who may have had past situations where no coaching or little coaching was provided. They may have strong feelings of abandonment or hopelessness that a program was not well supported.

Primary Focus Conversation

Select a program/initiative or a potential program/initiative that either is under way or could be added in your school or district. Select a program/initiative or a problem that is big, long-term, and/or has complicated moving parts.

(Continued)

(Continued)

Who will do the coaching? How often will coaching take place?

Continue the Conversation (Additional Prompts)

1. Have monies been set aside to provide ample coaching and on-the-job support for the program or initiative?

2. Have expectations been set to see the program put into practice?

3. What support loops have been set up to assist in the day-to-day bumps that can arise in implementing a new program?

Notes

DEEPER USE OF THIS CHAPTER: DEEPER DIVES

Fuel Source A: Extended Reflection

Answer the questions below in the context of your team, school, and/or district depending on the scope and responsibility of your task. Use the tools and reflections from this chapter to bring a greater depth to your team conversation. The questions below should be asked regarding any and all major initiatives, programs, or proposed solutions in your school or district.

Deeper Dive 7A—How are the right people going to be selected for the initial phases of implementation? What criteria will be used to aid in the selection?

Deeper Dive 7B—How will the selected people be trained for the new item(s) to be implemented? Who will do the training? How much training will be required for basic start-up?

Deeper Dive 7C—How will the trainees be provided ongoing coaching to support their learning and needs? Who will provide the coaching? How often will each person receive coaching support?

FUEL SOURCE B: THE RESOURCE OF LEADERSHIP

Background

Good things don't usually happen on their own. At least good things in organizations. Most often it takes preparation, dedication, and effort. Moreover, things that make a difference for students over a sustained period of time almost always fit in this category. Good sustained efforts that make a difference happen because dedicated people made it happen. Given that, it requires leadership and management to support these kinds of difference-maker efforts. Consider then, for a moment, the role that leadership and management must play to support these kinds of initiatives— initiatives that truly make a difference for students. One clear common denominator is activity. Leaders and managers in successfully driven initiatives are active. They are "in the middle" of the action at every step. They are constantly monitoring, observing, acquiring identified items, and supporting the process. Recall the maxim: Leaders lead people and managers manage things. Let's take a few moments and examine both sides of leadership and management.

Application Activity 7.4

Keep Things Moving (Management Leadership)

Recall the old saying "an army travels on its stomach." Those words are instructive for any manager. It takes things to keep initiatives moving. Food may be one thing, but consider all the "things" needed to support any major initiative. Materials, money, rooms, duty schedules, clerical support, schedules, and so on, and so on, and so on are just some of the materials that keep initiative fueled. And, for all of the things that you have, need, or want to be part of an initiative, someone has to monitor them all. In the same way a commanding army officer would never launch an offensive without all of the tactical and logistics support behind him or her, so it is with your initiative. Take time to carefully list, plot, and calendar which resources will be needed, by when, and the money to purchase them with. Further, continue the list by examining all of the logistics for things that don't need purchasing but do need managing. Think of things such as rooms, schedules, assignments, and other related items. List and plot all of these as well. Include all of the people who assist in the support of this management project. For an initiative to be successful, all of the "things" needed to fuel it as well as supporting the people who track all of the "things" must be looked after. It is the leader's task to keep this pipeline of fuel moving.

Application Activity 7.4

Keep Things Moving (Management Leadership)

Participants: Teams

Conversation Level: This Activity is not recommended for a beginning team (trust and foundational skill are needed first). But this is an excellent place to start with a team that is moving beyond the beginning stages of being a team. It is excellent for teams that are ready for a positive confidence-building conversation after basic team skills are present.

Purpose: This Activity is designed to have team members look at the broad picture of the programs and services they either provide now or are considering to include. This conversation helps the team members think through the logistics of materials and equipment and the rationale behind how they bring in and support a program. Be advised: These topics will likely bring out a broader look at what it takes to support a program or service. These conversations help a team realize that a new program or service will take a great deal of time and effort to get it to full implementation.

Goal: The goal of this discussion is for team members to recognize that having a process to discuss resources, materials, and equipment to install a new program is vital. Discussing the rollout plan is crucial for connectedness of the team.

Notes for Future Use: Keep notes on the efficacy of this Activity and the growth seen by team members. Take note of the ideas and suggestions given by the team. Vet these suggestions for applicability and practicality.

Primary Focus Conversation

Select a program/initiative or a potential program/initiative that either is under way or could be added in your school or district. Select a program/initiative or a problem that is big, long-term, and/or has complicated moving parts.

Who should be included to make an accurate accounting of the things needed to support and build the initiative in question?

Continue the Conversation (Additional Prompt)

1. What successes and struggles has the organization had in the past regarding having enough "things" to run the initiative as built?

Notes

IN ACTION: SUGGESTED USE

▶ *These prompts are built to provide a leader and a guiding team the conversation regarding selection of programs or evaluation of programs. These prompts are designed to bring out conversation to be sure that a selected program, idea, or solution is truly the best use of time, money, and energy, and that it is implemented well.*

Application Activity 7.5

Keep People Moving (Leadership Management)

People. It takes people. It takes smart, well-trained people. But, even when you have smart, well-trained and well-prepared people, issues arise. People are still people. They are variable. People are complicated, and their lives both inside and outside of work are complex. From time to time, people have static and changes in their lives that cause ripples through the work organization. People bring moods, feelings, concerns, and anxieties. All of these issues *must* be confronted and acknowledged by the leader. When people experience crisis or abrupt change in their lives, these ripples must be handled. The people must know they are cared about first, and then let the work ensue. Take time to acknowledge people and their changing lives. Running parallel to this is being able to read the anxiety and uncertainty levels as people attempt to implement the initiative. Be aware and be certain there are functioning feedback loops to transmit these feelings early and often.

Application Activity 7.5

Keep People Moving (Leadership Management)

Participants: Teams

Conversation Level: This Activity is not recommended for a beginning team (trust and foundational skill are needed first). But this is an excellent place to start with a team that is moving beyond the beginning stages of being a team. It is excellent for teams that are ready for a positive confidence-building conversation after basic team skills are present.

Purpose: This Activity is designed to have a team look at the broad picture of the programs and services they either provide now or are considering to include.

(Continued)

(Continued)

This conversation helps the team think through the need to account for the anxiety and unease that can come from team members when they are trying to implement new things. There must be a loop and recurring system to check on all members of the team for their emotional state. Be advised: These topics will likely bring out a broader look at what it takes to support a program or service. These conversations help a team realize that a new program or service will bring new feelings, anxieties, uncertainty, and insecurities. Using these conversations can help a team build trust and confidence that people will be taken care of, listened to, supported, and assisted.

Goal: The goal of this discussion is for team members to recognize that having a process to discuss their emotional state and readiness is critical. Having an outlet to know if the team is ready to handle more or deeper implementation is of the utmost importance. Clearly, there must be trust with the team that personal feelings can be safely shared.

Notes for Future Use: Keep notes on the efficacy of this Activity and the growth seen by team members. Take note of the ideas and suggestions given by the team. Vet these suggestions for applicability and practicality. Be careful to have a recurring system to revisit this topic often.

Primary Focus Conversation

Select a program/initiative or a potential program/initiative that either is under way or could be added in your school or district. Select a program/initiative or a problem that is big, long-term, and/or has complicated moving parts.

What systems and standing customs exist to care for the anxiety and feeling tone occurring around the initiative?

Continue the Conversation (Additional Prompts)

1. What are some successful examples of positive support around feeling tone that the organization has seen before?

2. What ideas does the group have to best care for the feelings of team members as time marches on?

Notes

DEEPER USE OF THIS CHAPTER: DEEPER DIVES

Fuel Source B: Extended Reflection

Answer the questions below in the context of your team, school, and/or district depending on the scope and responsibility of your task. Use the tools and reflections from this chapter to bring a greater depth to your team conversation. The questions below should be asked regarding any and all major initiatives, programs, or proposed solutions in your school or district.

> **Deeper Dive 7D**—Do leaders in the organization routinely provide good management of resources to keep programs and initiatives moving smoothly? What criteria are used to make this analysis?

> **Deeper Dive 7E**—Do leaders in the organization have the skill to provide leadership (of the people) when a program or initiative is undergoing change and instability? What criteria are used to make this analysis?

FUEL SOURCE C: THE SUPPORTS

Background

Programs don't run themselves. Further, programs don't monitor themselves. But, one can imagine that installing a program or initiative and never returning to observe whether or not it is working is a foolhardy notion. Much like a missile. There is an intended target determined before launch. So it is with a program or initiative. There is an intended target and desired outcome. One of the key aspects that takes place with any successful program is how the leader is able to monitor the in-the-moment data to make adjustments and read the success of the program. Again, think of the missile being launched. It would be laughable to imagine a military team launching a missile and then failing to monitor its flight and path. In fact, the real way this takes place is that after meticulous planning, once the missile is launched, it is monitored second-by-second by both computers and humans to carry out its precise mission. So it should be with our programs in our organizations. We should have systems and feedback loops that gather and display data in the moment about how a program is unfolding.

Application Activity 7.6

Gather, Collect, Assess

Think about how you know if things are or are not working in your organization. How reliable are the data to back this up? Are you left to fill in the missing pieces? How often do you get this actionable data? All too often, especially in educational organizations, we do not have good, solid data to monitor the progress of a program. There must be systems to gather data. In fact, it would be wise to investigate how often data can be reliably gathered. Ideally, there is a cross section of available data. Long-term data, mid-term data, and short-term data would be the best scenario. It would be up to the leader and team to decide the definitions of long-term, mid-term, and short-term. Another hallmark of a good system is that the data be easy to collect. All too often, teams and leaders will construct elaborate and complicated mechanisms to find data. But, what seems to happen over and over is that the plan collapses under its own weight. Things that are complicated and cumbersome lose steam quickly. Instead, push the team to think of simple, easy-to-access points of data especially for short- and mid-term analysis. Also, consider what the result targets are in advance. What should success look like? Be sure there is a "connect" between the plan, the data, the data gathering, and the assessment of the results. It takes time to map this out, but the time spent up front will be time saved in the confusion of a "lost" program, or worse, from a program that fades away into the scrap heap.

Application Activity 7.6

Gather, Collect, Assess

Participants: Teams

Conversation Level: This Activity is not recommended for a beginning team (trust and foundational skill are needed first). But this is an excellent place to start with a team that is moving beyond the beginning stages of being a team. It is excellent for teams that are ready for a positive confidence-building conversation after basic team skills are present.

Purpose: This Activity is designed to have team members look at the broad picture of the programs and services they either provide now or are considering to include. This conversation helps the team think through the need to account for data and measurement to demonstrate progress and targeted success. Be advised: These topics will likely bring out a broader look at what it takes to support a program or service. These conversations help a team realize that a new program or service will bring a need to monitor and measure it. Very often the conversation will spill over into other existing programs and services.

Goal: The goal of this discussion is for team members to recognize that having a process to discuss the need for data and measurement is of great importance. Most teams don't balk at the idea of monitoring per se, but they do struggle with coming up with a reasonable metric and system to regularly and routinely gather data.

Notes for Future Use: Keep notes on the efficacy of this Activity and the growth seen by team members. Take note of the ideas and suggestions given by the team. Vet these suggestions for applicability and practicality. Be careful to have a recurring system to revisit this topic often.

Primary Focus Conversation

Select a program/initiative or a potential program/initiative that either is under way or could be added in your school or district. Select a program/initiative or a problem that is big, long-term, and/or has complicated moving parts.

Do we have a system to collect data on the program or initiative?

Is it simple to use and simple to understand?

Have result targets been determined before the program launch?

Continue the Conversation (Additional Prompts)

1. Do the data gathered show short-, mid-, and long-term progress?

2. Are the targets flexible depending on the changes observed?

Notes

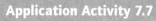

Application Activity 7.7

Feedback

Data must flow in multidirectional pathways. But, data are only data until they are converted into information. One of the most key pieces of information that any leader or organization can have is feedback. Feedback is a special kind of information. Feedback is best thought of as a purposeful, person-to-person, critical conversation. Feedback can be about people, things, or programs. Regardless, the feedback, its quality, and its timeliness is crucial. In terms of program monitoring, it is an imperative step that formal and informal feedback systems be established. Further, feedback systems require action on the part of both the receiver and the giver. The giver has the obligation to be sure the content of the feedback is accurate and necessary to share. The giver also bears the responsibility of maintaining the integrity of the feedback loop itself. This means the organization must hear from the leader that the feedback has been useful and the improvements that have come as a result. The usefulness of the feedback must be shared generally and anonymously. It is shared in terms of the program, not the people. The receivers have the responsibility to reflect and internalize the feedback. They must ask themselves how they can incorporate the feedback into their routines and actions. Giving the feedback its proper due can make a monumental difference in total performance. The leader must make it clear that giving and receiving feedback is an expectation.

Application Activity 7.7

Feedback

Participants: Teams

Conversation Level: This Activity is not recommended for a beginning team (trust and foundational skill are needed first). But this is an excellent place to start with a team that is moving beyond the beginning stages of being a team. It is excellent for teams that are ready for a positive confidence-building conversation after basic team skills are present.

Purpose: This Activity is designed to have team members look at the broad picture of the programs and services they either provide now or are considering to include. This conversation helps the team think through the need to account for feedback loops to share timely information about needs, successes, barriers, and collective next steps. Be advised: These topics will likely bring out a broader look at what it takes to support a program or service. These conversations help a team realize that a new program or service will bring a need to provide feedback to assess success and identify barriers.

Goal: The goal of this discussion is for team members to recognize that having a process to discuss the need for feedback is critical. Further, teams must have the security that if a team member bumps into a difficult or unique situation, there is a rapid and clear feedback loop to include others to facilitate prompt and appropriate action. This topic requires that the team has already worked through the sections and discussions on trust and conflict.

Notes for Future Use: Keep notes on the efficacy of this Activity and the growth seen by team members. Take note of the ideas and suggestions given by the team. Vet these suggestions for applicability and practicality. Be careful to have a recurring system to revisit this topic often.

Primary Focus Conversation

Select a program/initiative or a potential program/initiative that either is under way or could be added in your school or district. Select a program/initiative or a problem that is big, long-term, and/or has complicated moving parts.

What feedback systems exist in the organization now?

What feedback systems must be established to support the program or initiative?

Continue the Conversation (Additional Prompts)

1. What communication or training will have to take place to create and sustain feedback systems?

2. What preparations must be made to assist team members in understanding and trusting the feedback systems?

Notes

Application Activity 7.8

Systems and Barriers

Sometimes organizations get in their own way. Meaning, even though a new program or service arrives on the scene that is a great thing and solves an obvious need, there can often be hidden conflict. Some of the existing programs may unwittingly block or hamper the new program or initiative. It is critical that the leader and the team have regular discussions regarding this topic. What current systems seem to be in conflict with the new program? Further, what barriers have been discovered that must be eliminated, reduced, or neutralized? The learning leader and learning team must be constantly scanning the environment for this kind of information. There will always be other systems that do not mesh perfectly with a new program. This is also true of barriers discovered along the path. Things will appear that seem to "get in the way." This is normal. What happens next is what sets great organizations apart from average ones. Great organizations have established systems and standing mechanisms to bring these discoveries to those with the ability to clear the blockage.

Application Activity 7.8

Systems and Barriers

Participants: Teams

Conversation Level: This Activity is not recommended for a beginning team (trust and foundational skill are needed first). But this is an excellent place to start with a team that is moving beyond the beginning stages of being a team. It is excellent for teams that are ready for a positive confidence-building conversation after basic team skills are present.

Purpose: This Activity is designed to have team members look at the broad picture of the programs and services they either provide now or are considering to include. This conversation helps the team think through the need to account for the actions required from the feedback loops discussed in Application Activity 7.7. Be advised: These topics will likely bring out a broader look at what it takes to support a program or service. These conversations help a team realize that a new program or service will bring a need to provide feedback to assess success and identify barriers.

Goal: The goal of this discussion is for team members to recognize the importance of having a process to take action quickly and methodically from received feedback, especially when there is a barrier or blockage in a program or service. Team members have to have confidence that together and with the leader they are empowered to take action to fix identified issues.

Notes for Future Use: Keep notes on the efficacy of this Activity and the growth seen by team members. Take note of the ideas and suggestions given by the team. Vet these suggestions for applicability and practicality. Be careful to have a recurring system to revisit this topic often.

Primary Focus Conversation

Select a program/initiative or a potential program/initiative that either is under way or could be added in your school or district. Select a program/ initiative or a problem that is big, long-term, and/or has complicated moving parts.

What routines will have to be put in place to systematically discuss and handle discovered blockages and barriers?

Continue the Conversation (Additional Prompts)

1. Has the organization had past success in identifying and clearing barriers?

2. How will these behaviors become systems that can be maintained over time and examined for their effectiveness?

Notes

Application Activity 7.9

Performance

Having a great program or initiative is wonderful. It certainly beats the alternative, right? But, how do you know your program really is great? Can you prove it? Anything worth doing and putting a great deal of energy into is also worth measuring. There should be established targets of performance. These should be lofty enough to keep the team working and engaged but reachable enough to not cause discouragement. The learning leader and learning team should also establish measurements of performance along the way. Consider how "snapshots" can be taken of the program. In other words, there should be two kinds of data coming in: formative and summative. What formative pieces of data can be examined and shared with staff to show how things are happening in the moment? There should be expectations described as to how formative data can impact the short-term operations with the program. The long term is also very important. The leader and team should have set targets for long-term performance. Depending on the need, these targets could be half-year, full-year, or even multiyear. It is important that the team and staff know that the targets are set based on feedback and that they be reachable. It does no one any good to set performance targets that are either ridiculously easy or hard to reach. Revisit the discussion regarding performance targets often to be sure the team feels connected to them. Most important, the performance data allow for discussion about whether or not the program is working and achieving its desired claims.

Application Activity 7.9

Performance

Participants: Teams

Conversation Level: This Activity is not recommended for a beginning team (trust and foundational skill are needed first). But this is an excellent place to start with a team that is moving beyond the beginning stages of being a team. It is excellent for teams that are ready for a positive confidence-building conversation after basic team skills are present.

Purpose: This Activity is designed to have team members look at the broad picture of the programs and services they either provide now or are considering to include. This conversation helps the team think through the need to account for targets that are both summative and formative. The team should be comfortable setting targets that can shift based on current situations (formative) but that there is also a target that is looking at end-of-year success (summative). Be advised: These topics will likely bring out a broader look at what it takes to support a program or service. These conversations help a team realize that a new program or service will bring a need to provide feedback to assess success and identify barriers. This topic must be carefully monitored such that the team focuses on reasonable targets that are both lofty and attainable. The formative targets are a way for a team to function in the short term. These goals and targets can be short term in nature and based on the current actions in the classrooms or school. The bigger summative target can be a discussion to set year-to-year goals.

Goal: The goal of this discussion is for team members to recognize that having a process to set formative and summative targets is very important. A goal for a program or service has to have a big target, but there also has to be a series of incremental targets that the team can monitor to see success in the short term.

Notes for Future Use: Keep notes on the efficacy of this Activity and the growth seen by team members. Take note of the ideas and suggestions given by the team. Vet these suggestions for applicability and practicality. Be careful to have a recurring system to revisit this topic often.

Primary Focus Conversation

Select a program/initiative or a potential program/initiative that
either is under way or could be added in your school or district.
Select a program/initiative or a problem that is big, long-term,
and/or has complicated moving parts.

Are performance targets set that are both formative and summative?

Continue the Conversation (Additional Prompts)

1. How will the formative data be used?

2. How will summative data be used?

3. Has success been defined?

4. How often is the review of the program and its data going to take place?

Notes

DEEPER USE OF THIS CHAPTER: DEEPER DIVES

Fuel Source C: Extended Reflection

Answer the questions below in the context of your team, school, and/or
district depending on the scope and responsibility of your task. Use the
tools and reflections from this chapter to bring a greater depth to your
team conversation. The questions below should be asked regarding any
and all major initiatives, programs, or proposed solutions in your school
or district.

Deeper Dive 7F—Does the team have a system(s) in place to collect, analyze, and share data and information about a key program
or initiative? If not, why not? If so, what improvements are needed?

Deeper Dive 7G—How are leaders trained and supported to identify
barriers, obstacles, and impediments to success in a program or

initiative? Do leaders have permission to make corrections as they identify issues?

Deeper Dive 7H—Does the team function in a known "system," such that interconnected relationships are monitored for efficiency and performance? If not, what barriers must be addressed to establish this system? If so, what steps are regularly taken to test the system for smooth feedback loops?

Deeper Dive 7I—Does the team have a mechanism and system built to assess quality of implementation by practitioners based on the training and coaching received? If not, what barriers must be addressed to establish this system? If so, what steps are regularly taken to test the system for quality of performance?

CONCLUSION

Use the tools and reflections from this chapter to bring a greater depth to your team conversation. The questions and Application Activities in this chapter should be asked regarding any and all major initiatives, programs, or proposed solutions in your school or district.

Team Dynamics, Blunders, Traps, Directions, and Connecting Dots (the Pink Elephants)

8

Using This Chapter

This chapter is for leaders and learning teams who recognize that there are potential pitfalls and forces that can erode a team. These forces, if left unchecked, can cause teams to lose effectiveness, lose trust, and, in the extreme, lose their ability to function as a team. The most challenging nature of these forces are those that lurk unseen or under the surface.

If your team or team dynamics already functions very effectively and there are never any hidden agendas or hidden behaviors, then this chapter may not be the best use of your team's time.

It is highly recommended that readers using this chapter read the entire chapter first before using one of the Application Activities. This will give a background and perspective on the content and potential needs of the team.

INTRODUCTION

Of course your team is amazing. The members all perform at a Hall of Fame level on a daily basis. There is never any conflict. They all trust each other implicitly and explicitly. The norms of behavior are always followed without fail. The levels of performance exceed the targets in every measuring period. Every idea for tweaking and improving the system is based on data, thorough vetting, and research, and the ideas are not implemented without thoughtful consideration of the impact. The leader always provides clear direction and expectations. There is never any confusion or concern about where the destination lies. Further, the team never adds anything new without connecting it to the successful practices in the past.

I truly hope the paragraph above describes your team. I, however, am willing to bet that there are at least a handful of elements described above that don't exactly reflect your team. So, if my bet is correct, have no fear. You are normal and human. There is probably no such thing as the team described in the first paragraph above. It is an ideal state, to be sure. But, because we as humans are so variable, there is a chance that on any given day you may hit the ideal state in an area or two but slip out of that state in another. That's okay. Our efforts are all about the journey and not the destination. We hope to have continued improvement. We hope to have support for individuals. We hope to have a great place for students—all students—to learn, grow, and develop. But remember, hope is not a strategy or action step. It takes constant and consistent effort. It's a journey.

Along the way, however, there are some common potholes that we can be ever vigilant of. These common pitfalls are always there, and at any given time, your team might encounter one. The best thing one can do is to be watchful and observant. When you spot one of these issues, call attention to it and gather support to neutralize and overcome it. One thing for certain: Avoidance and ignoring these issues will not make them go away. Let's discuss some of the common bumps in the road.

Application Activity 8.1

Pink Elephants

One of the areas that must be confronted and addressed is the "pink elephants." O'Neil and Kulisek (2011) describe the giant, silent productivity killers on teams as "pink elephants." The pink elephants are in the room. They are always hanging around. The only way to get rid of them is to bring them out in the open and into the light of day. Teams must be willing and able to acknowledge that there are behaviors, customs, and actions that drain productivity. These pink elephants do not go away on their own. As long as they can survive and persist in the shadows, they will.

Teams, however, cannot hope to confront th[e]
having done the "pre-work" of building teams. Mea[n]
being able to get to the extermination of the pink ele[phants]
team on norms, trust, and an understanding of conflict. I[n]
ters, we examined the reason and purpose behind these imp[ortant]
It is a strong word of warning to not tackle the pink elephan[ts]
building a solid team foundation. But, one thing is certain: Until y[ou]
front the pink elephants that everyone notices but no one talks abou[t]
team will never move to a place of optimal performance. Be warned, ho[w-]
ever, the confrontation and exposure of pink elephants will almost certainly come with an emotional cost component. There will be many
feelings and nerve endings attached to the pink elephants. Removing
them will bring pain and upset. Tread lightly. Prepare for the possibilities.

Application Activity 8.1

Pink Elephants

Participant: Leader. Use the prompts below as the primary focus self-reflection. Make note of your responses.

Primary Focus Reflection

What foundational work must be done with the team before the discussion of pink elephants can take place?

If so, how much team building will have to take place in order to discuss the harmful nature of these pink elephants?

Continue the Reflection (Additional Prompts)

1. Will you (the leader) have to meet one-on-one with some team members to prepare them for the potential emotional flood that may ensue?

2. Is there reason to believe that some of the pink elephants may have quite a bit of maturity (age and time)?

Notes

pink elephants without
ning, the first steps in
hants is to build a
previous chap-
ortant pieces.
s without
ou con-
the

ty 8.2

:s

. Consider a baseball team. A
nate measure of the team will
another team. It is how they
eir skill and ability. But, just
ion where the coach (leader)
at, if corrected, would trans-
of play, yet not share it? In
should it be any different in
o receive feedback on their
more games?

..... elephants above, the discussion regarding performance brings feelings and nerve endings. These discussions cut close to the bone. One of the certain discoveries in discussing how teams perform and the dynamics between members is that observed substandard behaviors will likely be tied to the realization that things like this have gone on for long periods of time. Meaning, it is rare that people or teams suddenly slip into disarray and dysfunction. It is usually a slow slide. Teams and the dynamic between members or even the dynamic of how one team interacts with another is critical. Habits and behaviors must accelerate a team's performance. Things that inhibit performance must be identified and worked on.

Application Activity 8.2

Team Dynamics

Participant: Leader. Use the prompts below as the primary focus self-reflection. Make note of your responses.

Primary Focus Reflection

Are there observed dynamics either between team members or with other teams that may be inhibiting progress and performance?

Have any of these dynamics been around for a long period of time?

Continue the Reflection (Additional Prompts)

1. What team preparations will have to be made and put in place to address these team dynamics issues?

2. Are there any blocks or barriers that are certain to surface in trying to address and correct these issues?

3. How might these blocks or barriers be addressed?

Notes

Application Activity 8.3

The Blunders

Good decisions stemming from good ideas are clearly the ideal. The various activities in this book have been assisting you and your team in having a greater and greater probability of making great team decisions from great ideas. But, it is also instructive to look backwards to times when decisions didn't go well. What can we learn from the situations when decisions didn't go as planned?

Nutt (2002) describes the situations when decisions didn't go well as blunders. These blunders are usually made as a result of using failure-prone practices, such as making premature commitments to an idea or spending time and money on the wrong things (Nutt, 2002). Think about some of the decisions in your organization that didn't go well. Can you identify some of the characteristics listed above that may explain why things went the way they did? Remember, best practices are best practices, while other practices are not. We must know the difference between the two.

Application Activity 8.3

The Blunders

Participant: Leader. Use the prompts below as the primary focus self-reflection. Make note of your responses.

(Continued)

(Continued)

Primary Focus Reflection

Premature commitment to an idea is a failure-prone practice.
How can your team build in fail-safe practices to avoid premature
commitment to an idea?

What levels of participation will each member of the team have to bring to
prevent committing prematurely to an idea?

Continue the Reflection (Additional Prompt)

1. How does the team evaluate the spending of time and money to be sure they are going to the right things?

Notes

Application Activity 8.4

The Traps

Decisions from ideas are delicate things. As we discussed above, good decisions come from good practices. Good practices include having processes to discuss, vet, and examine ideas before committing to them. Once decisions and pathways are committed to, it is imperative that the decisions get off to a solid start. Nutt (2002) notes four critical evaluations to make regarding any fledgling idea/decision to avoid the traps that kill decisions. They are: ignoring barriers to action, lack of intervention or participation, providing ambiguous directions, and limited search for solutions.

Ignoring barriers is a form of living in denial. In a sense, it is using the notion that you hope things will get better or go away on their own. Remember, hope is not a strategy. Lack of participation is lethal in all its forms. Allowing team members to "pocket veto" a pathway is a form of passive aggression. People must participate at every step. Giving ambiguous directions creates confusion and disarray. Leaders must be clear on their steps to action, and team members are accountable to ask questions until they have clear understanding. Limited search for solutions is a certain death sentence to progress. Not moving to a thorough and complete search for possibilities is a form of surrender. Giving up and quitting early does not get a team anywhere. The exploration for the best solution may be difficult, but it is worth it.

Application Activity 8.4

The Traps

Participant: Leader. Use the prompts below as the primary focus self-reflection. Make note of your responses.

Primary Focus Reflection

Consider some big decisions you or your team have made in the last year. Can you think of one that was not a good decision or that didn't grow to its full potential?

Which of the four traps (ignoring barriers to action, lack of intervention or participation, providing ambiguous directions, and limited search for solutions) did it suffer from?

Continue the Reflection (Additional Prompt)

1. What part could members of the team play in preventing these same traps from reoccurring?

Notes

Application Activity 8.5

Ideas as Direction

Another fatal yet all too common flaw in the way ideas are generated as solutions to problems is the lack of connection to the vision and direction of the team. Meaning, the team members must have a direction *before* they generate ideas. There must be a target before problems are solved and solutions sought. The fatal flaw is the reverse of this, that is, when ideas arrive and the ideas become the target and direction. The ideas should feed and enhance the already determined direction, not the other way around.

Leaders and teams must have already accomplished the work of knowing what their goals and targets are long before problem solving and idea generation takes place. This way, teams are clear that the ideas being generated serve a specific purpose, but they don't change the overall target. Ideas should be generated for a focus and aimed at a purpose. Do not allow ideas to overtake and replace the target and direction of the team. Leaders must be certain that team members know the direction they are shooting for before they engage in idea generation. Teams must be clear about what their task is and how it fits into the larger picture and mission of the organization.

Further, be wary that ideas do not lead a team into "groupthink." Groupthink is where the team members agree to any idea or—worse—they take the first idea and mistake it for the best idea. Groupthink is also characterized by groups that don't disagree, especially with the leader, or don't have useful conflict with one another. This leads to "yes," but at a terrible cost. There is an idea and a decision, but there is no vetting and scrutiny given to the idea. The first idea becomes the action and solution. Beware of these scenarios.

Application Activity 8.5

Ideas as Direction

Participant: Leader. Use the prompts below as the primary focus self-reflection. Make note of your responses.

Primary Focus Reflection

Do the team members know the purpose their idea-finding and problem-solving are meant to achieve?

How has the team been prepared to know that there will be many ideas generated to solve a problem and that there will be a search to find the best one (not necessarily the first one)?

Continue the Reflection (Additional Prompt)

1. Do the team members know what their target, purpose, and direction are?

Notes

Application Activity 8.6

Connect the Dots

Everyone is entitled to his or her opinion and point of view. But, when it comes to team dynamics and good decision making, some voices are more important than others. Informed, current, and thoughtful experts should have the loudest and most-respected voice in the room. Decisions and direction should always be crafted from the input of those who are most current and most studied on a topic. A major consideration is taking the time as a team to connect the current state and position of the organization with how different paths will lead to particular outcomes.

> 🔑 **Key Thought**
>
> Informed, current, and thoughtful experts should have the loudest and most-respected voice in the room.

It is up to the leader and the team to understand that gathering input is only half the battle. Making all of the input and data surrounding a possible decision on an idea or direction into useful information is the real crux of the matter. Searching for input is critical, but keeping the team concentrated on the implications of the input and how it can influence a decision is the heart of all of this effort. Taking time as a team to debate the relationships between facts and their implications is where high-performing teams separate themselves from the pretenders. But take note: It is fruitless to have a debate if the team members don't have enough information to engage. It is the leader's responsibility to take time to bring the whole team up to speed on the needed information to thoroughly vet any decision.

Once teams have the right information and enough of it to have a quality examination of an idea, they will find that the idea will "click" in multiple directions. Good ideas bring more good ideas. Good ideas have self-expanding qualities (Young, 2009). Once the right path is found and selected, it will energize the team members, and they will find even greater possibilities. They will be eager to implement the idea and watch it make a difference. This reaction really comes only when ample time and deep discussion have occurred to find the best idea and the best path forward. Take time to save time.

Application Activity 8.6

Connect the Dots

Participant: Leader. Use the prompts below as the primary focus self-reflection. Make note of your responses.

Primary Focus Reflection

How is the team organized to give members time to search and find the background knowledge needed to thoroughly vet incoming ideas?

Continue the Reflection (Additional Prompts)

1. How will the team members know that they have found "enough" information to debate and evaluate an idea?

2. What team processes exist to drive conversation across all points of a proposed idea?

Notes

DEEPER USE OF THIS CHAPTER: DEEPER DIVES

The Pink Elephants: Extended Reflection—Deeper Dives 8A–8F

Leaders: Answer the questions below in the context of your team, school, and/or district depending on the scope and responsibility of your task. Use the tools and reflections from this chapter to bring a greater depth to your team conversation. The questions below should be asked regarding any and all major initiatives, programs, or proposed solutions in your school or district. This activity is not recommended for a leader just beginning work in this chapter. It is recommended that foundational work be done in this chapter first.

> **Deeper Dive 8A**—Team Dynamics. Is the team functional enough to discuss standing traditional behaviors and organizational norms? If not, what barriers are present that block the team from reaching this level of performance?

> **Deeper Dive 8B**—Pink Elephants. Is the team functional enough to discuss "giant silent productivity killers" (the pink elephants in the room)? If not, what barriers are present that block the team from reaching this level of performance?

> **Deeper Dive 8C**—The Blunders. How can premature commitments to ideas be avoided? How can every member of the team be tasked with resisting commitment to the first idea or solution suggested without fully vetting it for viability and quality?

> **Deeper Dive 8D**—The Traps. How is the team able to have meaningful conversation about the following traps: (1) ignoring barriers to action, (2) ambiguous direction, and (3) limited search for solutions? What barriers must be removed to allow the team the freedom to speak openly about concerns regarding these three traps?

> **Deeper Dive 8E**—Avoid Using Ideas as Direction. Is the team clear that setting a direction comes first and that ideas to achieve the direction come second? How do you know?

> **Deeper Dive 8F**—Ideas. Has the team been trained on the content needed to support the direction being targeted? Do suggested ideas connect to the target? How do you know?

CONCLUSION

Use the tools and reflections from this chapter to bring a greater depth to your team conversation. The questions and Application Activities in this chapter should be asked regarding any and all major initiatives, programs, or proposed solutions in your school or district.

Performance, Feedback, and Other Ways to Support, Maim, or Kill a Team (the Good, the Dangerous, and the Lethal)

9

Using This Chapter

This chapter is for leaders and learning teams who know that there are actions and repeated behaviors that can provide support and maintenance to teams. There is also a recognition that there are behaviors that can be destructive if allowed to persist and become habitual.

If your team or team dynamics has already come to a firm grasp of examining and exposing behaviors that are not conducive to team function, then this chapter may not be the best use of your team's time.

It is highly recommended that readers using this chapter read the entire chapter first before using one of the Application Activities. This will give a background and perspective on the content and potential needs of the team.

INTRODUCTION

At this stage of the book, you and your team are ready to tackle sustainability issues. Much like the analogy of buying a horse. Of course the first problem to solve is buying the horse. But, immediately following that moment comes the need to buy the hay to feed the horse, not to mention the corral and barn where she will spend her time. Water and access to veterinarian care will also enter the discussion. In other words, simply buying the horse is just the beginning. There are so many sustainability issues that come along with it. Learning leaders and learning teams would be wise to think of their programs much like buying a horse. The same sorts of sustainability issues must be solved to be sure all angles have been explored for optimal survival and quality of life.

Certainly, in many respects bringing a program or service to your school or district is much simpler than buying a living creature. But, in many other ways, it is much more complicated. Whenever there are groups of people who are involved in a situation, it always brings variables and wild cards. There are some considerations that are good rules of thumb to always address. Of course, there are more variables than any one book could ever address or give you strategies to overcome. But, this chapter will give you and your learning team some solid and practical issues to discuss and work through to be sure you are considering the real and present issues that can interrupt your sustainability efforts.

This chapter will look at things that support and sustain your efforts. These are the "good" things that learning leaders and learning teams should be doing. But, there is another side of the coin to keep in mind: There are "dangerous" and even "lethal" things that lurk out there that can derail and destroy all the good efforts you put in place. The dangerous and lethal issues discussed in the chapter also come with the antidote so that you and your team can account for and be aware of the actions that keep you safe and sound. Again, it should be mentioned that all of the things discussed in this chapter may not apply to you and your team's efforts at any given time. But, over time, these issues will surface. Be prepared. Take time to save time. Working through these conversations will prevent and expose weaknesses while things are small. Keep small things small. Use this chapter to keep things manageable and in control.

Application Activity 9.1

The Good: Selling the Idea: A Picture Is Worth 1,000 Words

Taking a page from the world of marketing and advertising, a business where everything depends on clear communication and messaging, we learn that anything that can be shown instead of told is always preferred. Don't give them a speech—give them a show (Arden, 2003). The brain attaches in a far more lasting way to the connection of a visual than to anything spoken. So, if your team is trying to make a deep connection to the rest of the school or organization, you should strongly consider developing a visual representation of your program, initiative, or service. Consider the power of the visual for some of your favorite brands of food or drink. Indeed, some of the visual representations of corporate logos are so familiar and recognizable that even in a different language, the brand is instantly identified.

Imagine if your program or service were easily connected to and identified. A visual connection could be just what is needed. Visuals, drawings, and pictures are often so much easier for people to connect to. They can understand the flow, direction, purpose, and personal connection so easily because it is represented rather than written or spoken. It may take some real time, brainpower, and creativity, but the payoff can be huge.

Application Activity 9.1

The Good: Selling the Idea: A Picture is Worth 1,000 Words

Participants: Teams

Conversation Level: This can be a moderate- to high-level conversation for a team. This level of discussion is not typically a good one for a newly formed team. It is best for teams to have some success working together first before exploring this topic.

Purpose and Groundwork: This Activity is designed to have a team look at the importance of representing a program, service, or initiative in graphic, diagram, or visual form. Many times there are team members or especially others outside of the team who will have to understand the work of the team. One of the most efficient methods to communicate with others is with a picture, graphic, or diagram. This delivery method is far less likely to have errors than using spoken words alone. Be advised: These topics will likely bring out a broader look at what it takes to support a program or service. These conversations help a team realize that a new program or service can benefit greatly by having a picture or representation to quickly describe and show people what the team is working on. This topic must be carefully monitored such that the team focuses on the program and its true purpose. Capturing the program visually should be carefully done to be sure the communication is comprehensible. It is wise to consider sharing the proofs of the work to some key staff members who have artistic or visual talents. Vet the visual with them to be sure it is truly communicating what it is meant to.

(Continued)

(Continued)

Goal: The goal of this discussion is for team members to recognize that having a visual is a very important and efficient way for a program to be communicated to those who may not be familiar with it. Share the proofs with the team to be sure all members understand the visual and have added their two cents along the way.

Notes for Future Use: Keep notes on the efficacy of this Activity and the growth seen by team members. Take note of the ideas and suggestions given by the team. Vet these suggestions for applicability and practicality. Be careful to have a recurring system to revisit this topic often.

Primary Focus Conversation

What elements of your initiative or program can be represented visually?
What things can be captured as a flowchart or step by step?

Continue the Conversation (Additional Prompts)

1. What parts of your program will require a little or a lot of creativity to represent them visually?

2. How difficult will it be to "show" the entire program in a visual?

Notes

IN THE SCHOOL

▶ *Madison Elementary School—The principal used this conversation with her Leadership Team. She wanted to bring out as much creativity as possible around their schoolwide math goal.*

Application Activity 9.2

The Good: Communication and Frequency

Communication is key. This is certainly not an unfamiliar idea. It is easy to imagine that the absence of good communication is a certain disaster and demise for any program. So, we know that communication is necessary. But, do we stop to consider the method of communication? Do you have the discussion with the learning team about *how* we communicate? When was the last time the team was queried about the effectiveness of their communication? Was everyone connected? Are segments of the organization or larger community being missed? Why?

One key idea to discuss with the team is "frequency theory." Frequency theory suggests that we all emit our own unique frequency in our everyday lives (Belsky, 2010). As we stretch to communicate with people at other frequencies, we must adjust how we communicate, present our ideas, and engage others—meaning everyone is tuned to their own private radio station. People have different backgrounds, levels of receptivity, preparedness, and levels of concern. These things and more can determine the "radio station" or "frequency" they are tuned to.

Using the idea of frequency theory means that a leader and team have to understand that communication about a program or initiative will have to be sent out in *many* ways. Think about your own preferences to receive communication. You may be a person who is tethered to your smartphone or device. Communication for you may be dominated by things that come through your device. What if an important update for your workplace *didn't* come through as a communication on your device? You might miss it entirely. What if you are a person who likes paper or e-mail or some other vehicle? But now, the wrench for a team is to have a mechanism to communicate in as many ways as you can think of, because some people's "stations" are tuned to one thing and some are tuned to another. The best leaders and teams know that their message has to be tailored to the receiver. It's not about making the receiver come to you. The message has to be given so that others can get it wherever they are and however they prefer.

Application Activity 9.2

The Good: Communication and Frequency

Participants: Teams

Conversation Level: This can be a moderate- to high-level conversation for a team. This level of discussion is not typically a good one for a newly formed team. It is best for teams to have some success working together first before exploring this topic.

(Continued)

(Continued)

Purpose and Groundwork: This Activity is designed to have a team look at the importance of sharing and providing updates about the program. This communication is critical that it occur in a variety of ways. The program must have proper and effective communication to be sure all stakeholders know why the program is important and the intended targets. Be advised: These topics will likely bring out a broader look at what it takes to support a program or service. These conversations help a team realize that a new program or service can benefit greatly by having multiple and varied communication methods to keep the school community connected. This topic must be carefully monitored such that the team focuses on the program and its true purpose. Capturing the program through communication methods is important. The delivery is almost as important as the message. Be aware of how all stakeholders like to receive communication. Be sure that all the methods are used.

Goal: The goal of this Activity is for team members to recognize that having a clear and varied communication delivery is of utmost importance. Further, it is crucial that the team continually discuss the methods of communication to be sure the stakeholders are being reached in the most effective way for them.

Notes for Future Use: Keep notes on the efficacy of this Activity and the growth seen by team members. Take note of the ideas and suggestions given by the team. Vet these suggestions for applicability and practicality. Be careful to have a recurring system to revisit this topic often.

Primary Focus Conversation

What challenges will you have getting the message out in the variety of ways needed to keep everyone informed and up to date?

Continue the Conversation (Additional Prompts)

1. How has the team studied the targets for communication?

2. What methods does the community favor to receive communication?

Notes

IN THE SCHOOL

▶ *Washington High School—The principal used this conversation with her Leadership Team. She wanted the team to be alert to the many 21st century methods of communication available to connect to all school stakeholders.*

Application Activity 9.3

The Good: Ingredients of the High-Performing Team

High-performing teams exhibit particular behaviors. They come with observable characteristics. They exhibit these characteristics because they find over time that in order to sustain their high performance there are certain states of mind and states of behavior that allow them to routinely perform well. The basic four characteristics of high-performing teams can be grouped into the following descriptors: (1) context, (2) composition, (3) competencies, and (4) change management skills (Dyer, Dyer, & Dyer, 2013).

Dyer and colleagues (2013) describe "context" as defined performance goals. Further, these goals must come with reward systems, information systems, human resource practices, and supportive culture for team work. In other words, performance goals can't be set in isolation. Goals must stretch across the organization to impact everyone—hence the need for practices that are beyond the team and are seen by other departments. This means that top management must understand and support the goals being set by teams. Coordination is king.

> ### 🔑 Key Thought
>
> Goals must stretch across the organization to impact everyone.

The people on the team make the difference. Dyer and colleagues (2013) note that individual team members must be examined as to their personal skill to be on the team. What do they bring? Do they have the technical skill to be on the team? What communication and interpersonal skills do team members bring? Is the team size appropriate to get their tasks accomplished? Do team members have the motivation and energy to accomplish the task? These questions must be asked and answered. Who you put in the room matters. It matters greatly. Don't simply convene a team because it has always been done that way. Make teams come together because they have the right people and a meaningful task. Start there.

Teams must be able to articulate their goals and metrics. More important, the team must be able to clearly articulate the means to be used to accomplish their goals (Dyer et al., 2013). Team members must understand their assignments, their role, and the purpose of the team. It is also crucial to take time as a team to do team building, trust building, and conflict discussion. Team members must also understand from the leader that risk taking and innovation are welcome. This is an area where feedback among team members and the leader is crucial.

Change and the ability to understand and manage change are critical parts of a team's success. Teams must be able to monitor themselves and monitor the needs of the organization (Dyer et al., 2013). Taking careful observations of the needs allows the team to discuss changes, alterations, and shifts. Teams must have time and background in how to handle and effectuate change. The point of managing change is to allow for processes to continuously improve. This is a difficult step for teams, and yet one of the most important.

Application Activity 9.3

The Good: Ingredients of the High-Performing Team

Participants: Teams

Conversation Level: This can be a moderate- to high-level conversation for a team. This level of discussion is not typically a good one for a newly formed team. It is best for teams to have some success working together first before exploring this topic.

Purpose: This Activity is designed to have a team look at the importance of being sure that all team members understand their task and assignment. The purpose of this discussion is for a team to understand why it is always important for a team to restate their assigned tasks for understanding and so that other members know exactly what is asked of each member. Be advised: These topics will likely bring out a broader look at what it takes to support a program or service. These conversations help a team realize that a new program or service can benefit greatly by having a clear and stated set of tasks for each team member.

Goal: The goal of this discussion is for team members to recognize that having a clear task delineation is crucial to the success of any program. It is important that every meeting have a clear communication about what is expected and what each member is asked to do.

Primary Focus Conversation

Does the team understand their task? Does the team have goals related to the task? Does the team understand that continuous improvement is the overarching goal?

Continue the Conversation (Additional Prompts)

1. Are the right people on the team?

2. Have people been trained to be on the team?

Notes

IN THE SCHOOL

▶ *Madison Elementary School—The principal used this conversation with her Leadership Team. She wanted to help build the team by examining the importance of goals, continuous improvement, having the right people involved in the task, and training.*

Application Activity 9.4

The Dangerous: Planning Mistakes

The saying "failing to plan is planning to fail" exists for a reason. Whether you've lived this in your personal life or professional life, it leaves a lasting impression one way or the other. Like the time as a child you forgot to pack a toothbrush for an overnight camping trip or something with more consequence at work, these things can almost always be traced back to poor planning and preparation. Even minor oversights and inconveniences can be linked back to faulty systems and faulty planning.

In the workplace, faulty planning is a dangerous thing. It is dangerous to the health of any program or initiative. Planning takes time. Planning takes leadership. Planning requires effort and observational skills. Schmidt (2009) notes that there are six dangerous planning mistakes: (1) tolerating vague objectives, (2) ignoring environmental context, (3) using limiting tools and process, (4) neglecting stakeholder interests, (5) one-shot planning, and (6) mismanaging people dynamics. Consider each of the six dangerous planning mistakes. Each one is common and each one exists in plain sight. None of the six is tricky or hard to observe. But, one thing they all have in common is that they each require effort on the part of the leader and team to take the time and effort to neutralize them.

The Good: Solutions to the Dangerous Planning Mistakes

There are six solutions to the dangerous planning mistakes listed above (adapted from Schmidt, 2009):

1. Be sure objectives are clear and measurable; be sure the team takes time to define and understand the *why* before *what* and *how;*

2. Understand internal and external threats; take care to identify risks, weak spots, likely points of failure, and possible solutions for each item; make, test, manage, and monitor assumptions;

3. Choose and use a common and agreed-upon planning model; stick to the process; modify when needs arise, but don't abandon the process;

4. Build and broaden your team—expand the communication of your program to the entire organization; people support what they create and understand;

5. Keep the process fluid; refine your steps continuously; use cycles such as "think, plan, act, assess"; and

6. Celebrate successes; search for success at every turn; be sure to check in emotionally with people involved in the program regularly and often.

The real place where the rubber meets the road for a learning leader and a learning team is taking the time and effort to identify any of the six dangerous planning mistakes. Further, it takes dedicated effort to question and examine the team and organization to determine what exists, what shouldn't exist, and what should be overcome. But, consider the power that team members can possess when they have such mastery over their environment that they can scan and evaluate across any and all of these six areas. It means that a team truly has the ability and skill to look at anything in the organization to evaluate the benefit or detriment of anything. This is a place of ultra-high performance. Teams don't start here. They earn their way here. Take the time to build a team in the earlier chapters to one day arrive here. But, just imagine the results a team functioning at this level could see!

Application Activity 9.4

The Dangerous: Planning Mistakes

Participants: Teams

Conversation Level: This can be a moderate- to high-level conversation for a team. This level of discussion is not typically a good one for a newly formed team. It is best for teams to have some success working together first before exploring this topic.

Purpose: This Activity is designed to have a team look at the implications and importance of planning. This is a high-level conversation for teams that are established and functioning. Do not hold this conversation with a team that is not yet displaying trust and the ability to share objectively. This topic is meant to impress on a team that planning and preparation are paramount to sustained success. Be advised: These topics will likely bring out a broader look at what it takes to support a program or service. These conversations help a team realize that a new program or service will bring a need to discuss planning and contingencies from many angles.

Goal: The goal of this discussion is for team members to recognize that having a process to discuss planning and the need to be prepared is the point. Planning requires all members of the team to pitch in and share their vantage points. The conclusion of this topic is for team members to be committed to planning and revisiting their plan often to discuss viability.

Notes for Future Use: Keep notes on the efficacy of this Activity and the growth seen by team members. Take note of the ideas and suggestions given by the team.

(Continued)

(Continued)

Vet these suggestions for applicability and practicality. Be careful to have a recurring system to revisit this topic often.

Primary Focus Conversation

What success have the leader and team had with planning in the past?

What have been some examples of when things were not
as well planned as they could have been?

Continue the Conversation (Additional Prompts)

1. Can you identify which of the planning mistakes was in effect?

2. What could have been done differently to avoid this situation?

Notes

IN THE SCHOOL

▶ *Jefferson Middle School—The principal used this reflection with his Leadership Team. He used these prompts because he wanted to build a transparent culture so that past mistakes could be acknowledged and used as a learning experience.*

Application Activity 9.5

The Lethal: Lack of Feedback, Feedback, Feedback

Ideas are great. Ideas can bring energy, attention, and excitement. But, ideas must have certain ingredients to grow to full maturity. Just like plants require carbon dioxide, sunlight, water, and soil, ideas, too, require elements to help them grow. One of the most important elements to enable ideas to grow into something that can create change is feedback (Belsky, 2010). Ideas take on a life of their own when they are shared, and especially so when feedback is sought and used.

Think back across your experiences. Can you reflect on a time when a program or initiative was very successful in your school or district? Think about the channels of feedback that were built or used. Successful programs have feedback loops. Skilled leaders and teams find ways, both formal and informal, to gather feedback from all directions. Take another moment and reflect on a program that you were part of that was installed but had no feedback systems. Think about the deterioration and breakdown that eventually ensued. How might feedback or more regular feedback have helped prevent this?

Feedback is critical. Just like flying an airplane, one wouldn't expect a pilot to simply get the plane off the ground then never look at the dials, instruments, and computer data, right? I don't think any of us would want to be a passenger on that plane. So it should be with the programs we install in our schools. There should be plenty of "in flight" data that we can listen to, gather, and discuss. Gather feedback. Don't fly the plane blind.

> ### 🔑 Key Thought
>
> Feedback is critical. Just like flying an airplane, one wouldn't expect a pilot to simply get the plane off the ground then never look at the dials, instruments, and computer data, right?

The Good: Solutions to the Lethal Lack of Feedback

Make it simple. There is nothing about feedback that has to be a difficult and gigantic monster. Feedback can be both formal and informal. Formal feedback could be the end-of-year reports, program evaluation meetings with a supervisor, or budget reconciliation reports. Informal could be anecdotal conversation passed from person to person, observation and description, and site visit reports and sharing.

Keep the conversation useful and simple. Take time to help the team know that we really only need three pieces of feedback on a regular basis: what to *start* doing, what to *stop* doing, and what to *continue* doing (Belsky, 2010). Imagine if all the conversations you have with your team about programs channeled into these three action points. Can you imagine the power? A team member shares feedback and the team helps categorize the feedback into one of the three areas. The feedback suddenly changed from something overheard, observed, or monitored into something actionable. This can push a team into a constant drive to be action oriented. It will also push a team to crave feedback. Information is king.

Application Activity 9.5

The Lethal: Lack of Feedback, Feedback, Feedback

Participants: Teams

Conversation Level: This can be a moderate- to high-level conversation for a team. This level of discussion is not typically a good one for a newly formed team. It is best for teams to have some success working together first before exploring this topic.

Purpose: This Activity is designed to have a team look at the importance of having systems of feedback that function and repeat. This is a high-level conversation for a team because it asks a team to think of a past successful activity and the feedback loops that existed. Feedback and identifiable loops of feedback are critical to a program's success. These conversations will anchor this point.

Goal: The goal of this discussion is for team members to recognize that having a system for feedback and the loops of feedback is where the team should land. It is important for the leader that the team not get bogged down thinking of past challenges in this area. Instead, focus on what can be done to improve or tighten the systems.

Notes for Future Use: Keep notes on the efficacy of this Activity and the growth seen by team members. Take note of the ideas and suggestions given by the team. Vet these suggestions for applicability and practicality. Be careful to have a recurring system to revisit this topic often.

Primary Focus Conversation

Reflect on a time when a program or initiative was very successful in your school or district. Think about the channels of feedback that were built or used. How did feedback play a role in keeping this program successful?

Notes

IN THE SCHOOL

▶ *Jefferson Middle School—The principal used this reflection with his Leadership Team. He used these prompts because he wanted the team to have a discussion regarding past successes and the role that feedback played. He wanted to build trust and team dynamics so that feedback can be a regular and expected tool.*

Application Activity 9.6

The Lethal: Mistaken Assumptions of People and Meetings

We all know that the meetings in your organization are fabulous (wink, wink). It's the meetings going on in other schools or departments that are bland, boring, and unproductive, right? Are you sure? How do you know?

Meetings are a reflection of the productivity of the team. Meetings that are unidirectional (leader to members) are often either a chance to "pound the pulpit" or "deliver trivia recitals." Pounding the pulpit may seem productive to leaders because they "told them" and the audience will be motivated by their words alone. This is rarely the case. The other style is to use a meeting to exchange trivial information, directions, or instructions. These meetings are dreadful and lead to people reaching for their electronic device as quickly as possible to escape mentally from this horrid waste of time.

Bens (2005) reminds us of a few things about the assumptions of meetings that are killers: (1) people want to be at the meeting; (2) everyone is clear on the purpose of the meeting; (3) there are no distractions, baggage, or historical precedents blocking participation; and (4) the people at the meeting are appropriately empowered to make decisions and act on agenda items. Leaders or facilitators who walk into a meeting not keeping these four simple things in mind could be unwittingly eroding team function and capacity by the minute. Think about you and the meetings you attend. Don't these four items ring rather loudly as things you wish were either reversed or eliminated?

Poor use of time with a meeting is a real momentum killer for teams. Leaders and facilitators have to examine this reality often. Most of the time, people are compliant enough to attend. But, if you ask them, you will learn that time and experience have taught them to have a low expectation of productivity from meetings. For initiatives and programs to work and be sustainable, meetings must be productive.

> **Key Thought**
>
> Poor use of time with a meeting is a real momentum killer for teams.

The Good—Juggling the People: Solutions to Lethal Mistaken Assumptions of Meetings

There are some simple and some not so simple fixes to some of the trouble spots listed above. Some of the simple beginning steps are (1) have an agenda, (2) put a time/duration limit on each agenda item or group, (3) take scheduled breaks and put them on the agenda, (4) start and end on time—no matter what, and (5) assign roles (facilitator, timekeeper, recorder, process observer, to name a few).

On the more complicated side, work toward getting the group to shift from *what* conversations to *how* (away from content and instead talk process) (Bens, 2005). This is something that takes conscious effort. It is all too easy for teams to debate and fuss around about the *what*. But, getting them to channel the conversation to *how* things can be done, improved, or streamlined, suddenly the meeting takes on a much more productive tone. *How* leads to actionable steps. *What* just opens the door to grousing around. Beware. Also, the leader or facilitator of the group has to recognize that many groups often attempt to deal with an unrealistic number of items, which causes members to scramble from topic to topic (Bens, 2005). Build a process to limit the number of items. Find a sorting process to screen items to keep only the most important things on the actual "go to meeting" agenda. Allow the team to submit items knowing that only the most pressing will actually make the final agenda.

> **Key Thought**
>
> It is all too easy for teams to debate and fuss around about the *what*. But, getting them to channel the conversation to *how* things can be done, improved, or streamlined, suddenly the meeting takes on a much more productive tone.

Many meetings are designed without paying attention to the process of exactly how each agenda item will be handled (Bens, 2005). It is the task of the leader to be sure the facilitator knows and has a process planned to handle every item on the agenda. Just like good teaching, there should be a variety of grouping and discussion activities to get the attendees involved, moving, and talking. The whole point is to make the meeting a place where brainpower comes out. If people are sitting, static, and disengaged, you are sunk. Build processes to engage and activate. Also, be aware that any time a decision or conclusion has to be reached by the group it is the task of the facilitator to have a process selected to help the group, reach a fair and understood decision.

Application Activity 9.6

The Lethal: Mistaken Assumptions of People and Meetings

Participant: Leader. Use the prompts below as the primary focus self-reflection. Make note of your responses.

Primary Focus Reflection

Does every meeting have a built agenda with times? Does every agenda have a prepared process to handle each item and each decision? Does the agenda have activity and conversation times built in?

Continue the Reflection (Additional Prompts)

Does the leader or facilitator have a feedback loop to ask members what about the meeting worked or didn't work for them?

1. If any of these are not present, take the time to install them.

2. As a leader or as a team, are there misconceptions about meetings and their purpose?

3. How are meetings being checked for their usefulness?

4. How are team members queried about their thoughts on how meetings would work better for them?

Notes

CONCLUSION

Use the tools and reflections from this chapter to bring a greater depth to your team conversation. The questions and Application Activities in this chapter should be asked regarding any and all major initiatives, programs, or proposed solutions in your school or district.

Leadership, Support, Structure, and Conclusion 10

LEADERSHIP

This work and these efforts do not happen spontaneously. These conversations happen because someone moved the group to do it. These changes take place because someone had the courage to take on the habits of the past. It takes a learning leader to point the team in a direction. Leaders bring the confidence that the journey is worth taking and that there is a destination in mind.

It takes someone to get the team moving in a common direction. It takes someone to communicate and make the decision. It takes someone to have the crucial conversations with team members who may struggle or have challenges in embracing the new pathways. It will take courage and determination. But, once a leader starts this journey, it becomes obvious that there is no point returning to the place you came from. The new world of better performance, better team dynamics, better student performance, and better climate is too invigorating to let go. So, as the leader, make the commitment. Start the journey. Take your team with you. It will be the best decision you ever made.

SUPPORT

Keep a close eye on the dynamics of the team. Watch and listen for members who may struggle from time to time. Help them. Talk with them. Seek to understand what they are going through. Provide encouragement. Keep people connected. Don't let any team members feel like they are alone.

Value the input and interchange from team members along the way. Remember, there is no way to predict where any given team will go. Some teams get stuck in a place where other teams don't even blink at that location. Enjoy the unpredictability. Keep the conversations moving. Keep the tasks productive. Just keep moving. Stay focused. Support vital behaviors. Celebrate victories.

STRUCTURE—THE OVERALL STRUCTURE: THE FIRST 15 MINUTES, THE NEXT 45 MINUTES

This book has taken an intense focus on basically the first 15 minutes of a meeting. The point and purpose is to build the team, build trust, create capacity, spur creativity, address problems, and even celebrate progress and success. It should come to mind, however, that if a meeting lasts 60 minutes and the first 15 are covered, then how do the leader and the team ensure that the remaining 45 minutes are well structured, cohesive, and productive?

The next area of focus that will be considered in future work will be how to create a structure for principals to use for organization that will create a dynamic for long-term solutions—meaning, there are many structuring devices and team systems that help teams focus on student work and instructional strategies. But, there are few, if any, systems to anchor the school and teams to a three- to five-year cohesive structure. Further, there is nothing that makes the connection between the need for trust and team building to then connect to a structure where the teachers and staff have a value, voice, and vested interest in creating a great school and a great place to come to work every day. This will be the next piece to focus on.

CONCLUSION

Mama said there would be days like this. We've all had them. Every leader and team has them. The rough day. The rough meeting. The flat result. Something. The curve ball. Don't fret.

The real question isn't how to avoid the bumpy day. Remember the wise old saying, "Smooth seas never built a skilled sailor." The real question, therefore, is: "How will you react and still keep your target in view?" Once effort and sustained focus are given to a project, it is always disappointing when progress is slowed down. But, when it happens, and it will, remember to step back and take stock. Look back at the success had to date. Look back at the ground already covered. Look back at the growth. Take time to reflect on the celebrations.

After you've reflected, then stop to ask what the temporary setback may mean. Don't ever assume that the explanation can mean only that the airplane is in a death spiral dive and there is no way to pull out of it. This is rarely the case. The death spiral doesn't "just appear." In real schools with real people, it takes time for disintegration to set in. So, don't allow your thoughts to spin off into this place.

Consider all the possibilities and then look for the variables you can control. Begin to look at things one at a time. Don't try to understand the whole forest. Study one tree at a time. Learn all you can about that one single tree. Look at the details. Look at the things and people that are connected to that single thing. Find the positives. Find the next steps. Find the next most logical step for success.

Shift the routines. Make things operate differently. Give people a new setting or task to shift their focus. Sometimes by looking away from the thing that is causing the glare and then returning to it, you are able to see it more clearly. Help team members take a temporary hiatus from the task. Take the spotlight off it. Allow it to come back in a less obvious and center-stage fashion.

Things such as ambiguity and perceived failure will pop up from time to time. As a learning leader and as a learning team, it is important to recognize ambiguity and talk openly about it. Ambiguity becomes a killer when it is allowed to live in the shadows and hunt like a camouflaged sniper. But, when ambiguity is brought out into the light of day and talked about, it helps people cope with the uncertainly. It helps people know that they are not alone. People respond to ambiguity in personal ways. Look for it. The same goes for perceived failure. Do not, under any circumstance, allow team members to define failure on their own. The targets for results are the responsibility of the whole team. Just because some bumps in the road appear and some might perceive it as failure, it is important that the team addresses this. Just like a sports team that is losing at halftime, there is still plenty of game left to play. Anything can happen. It will take focus, but it certainly isn't impossible. Look for the positives. Look for the next steps that will bring success.

Always remember what you're doing this for. This is about a belief that more students can learn and learn deeply. This is about a belief that more students can reach higher than they have before. This is about a belief that teachers can reach more students. This about a belief that really well-trained teachers—organized into teams, given a clear common purpose, and with the resources needed—can work miracles. Believe it.

You can do it.

References

Arden, P. (2003). *It's not how good you are, it's how good you want to be.* New York, NY: Phaidon.

Belsky, S. (2010). *Making ideas happen: Overcoming the obstacles between vision & reality.* New York, NY: Portfolio/Penguin.

Bens, I. (2005). *Advanced facilitation strategies: Tools & techniques to master difficult situations.* San Francisco, CA: Jossey-Bass.

Brinson, D., & Steiner, L. (2007, October). *Building collective efficacy: How leaders inspire teachers to achieve* (Issue Brief, pp. 1–6). Washington, DC: The Center for Comprehensive School Reform and Improvement.

Cloke, K., & Goldsmith, J. (2000). *Resolving conflicts at work: A complete guide for everyone on the job.* San Francisco, CA: Wiley.

Dyer, W. G., Jr., Dyer, J. H., & Dyer, W. G. (2013). *Team building: Proven strategies for improving team performance* (5th ed.). San Francisco, CA: Jossey-Bass.

Fixsen, D., & Blase, K. (2015). *Implementation drivers.* The National Implementation Research Network. Retrieved from http://nirn.fpg.unc .edu//sites/implementation.fpg.unc.edu/files/NIRN-ImplementationDrivers AssessingBestPractices.pdf

Fullan, M., & Quinn, J. (2016). *Coherence: The right drivers in action for schools, districts, and systems.* Thousand Oaks, CA: Corwin.

Glei, J. K. (Ed.). (2013). *Manage your day-to-day: Build your routine, find your focus & sharpen your creative mind* (Vol. 1). Las Vegas, NV: Amazon.

Haren, F. (2006). *The idea book.* Stockholm, Sweden: Interesting Books.

Hattie, J. (2009). *Visible learning: A synthesis of over 800 meta-analyses relating to achievement.* New York, NY: Routledge.

Hattie, J. (2012). *Visible learning for teachers: Maximizing impact of learning.* New York, NY: Routledge.

Hattie, J. (2015, October). *Keynote address.* Presented at the California Visible Learning Institute, Universal City, CA.

Hess, F. M. (2013). *Cage-busting leadership.* Cambridge, MA: Harvard Education Press.

Kelley, C. J., & Shaw, J. J. (2009). *Learning first!: A school leader's guide to closing achievement gaps.* Thousand Oaks, CA: Corwin.

Lencioni, P. (2005). *Overcoming the five dysfunctions of a team: A field guide.* San Francisco, CA: Jossey-Bass.

Nutt, P. C. (2002). *Why decisions fail: Avoiding the blunders and traps that lead to debacles.* San Francisco, CA: Berrett-Koehler.

O'Neil, S., & Kulisek, J. (2011). *Bare knuckle people management: Creating success with the team you have—Winners, losers, misfits, and all.* Dallas, TX: BenBella Books.

Rath, T., & Conchie, B. (2008). *Strengths based leadership: Great leaders, teams and why people follow.* New York, NY: Gallup Press.

Schmidt, T. (2009). *Strategic project management made simple: Practical tools for leaders and teams.* Hoboken, NJ: John Wiley & Sons.

Sinek, S. (2009). *Start with why: How great leaders inspire everyone to take action.* New York, NY: Portfolio/Penguin.

Stanier, M. B. (2010). *Do more great work.* New York, NY: Workman.

Van Doren, C. (1991). *A history of knowledge: Past, present, and future.* New York, NY: Ballantine.

Wiseman, L., Allen, L., & Foster, E. (2013). *The multiplier effect: Tapping the genius inside our schools.* Thousand Oaks, CA: Corwin.

Young, J. W. (2009). *A technique for producing ideas.* West Valley City, UT: Waking Lion Press.

Index

A SAGE Publishing Company

Solutions you want. Experts you trust. Results you need.